I0423699

PRESIDENT'S MALARIA INITIATIVE

Liberia

Malaria Operational Plan FY 2016

TABLE OF CONTENTS

ABBREVIATIONS and ACRONYMS

ACT	Artemisinin-based combination therapy
ANC	Antenatal care
BCC	Behavior change communication
CDC	Centers for Disease Control and Prevention
CHT	County health team
CSH	Collaborative Support for Heath
CY	Calendar year
DHS	Demographic and Health Survey
DHIS	District Health Information System
DTS	Dried blood tube sample
EUV	End-use verification
EVD	Ebola virus disease
FARA	Fixed Amount Reimbursement Agreement
FY	Fiscal year
gCHV	General community health volunteer
GHI	Global Health Initiative
Global Fund	Global Fund to Fight AIDS, Tuberculosis and Malaria
GOL	Government of Liberia
HCW	Health care worker
HFS	Health facility survey
HMIS	Health Management Information System
iCCM	Integrated community case management
IEC	Information, education, communication
IMCI	Integrated management of childhood illnesses
IPTp	Intermittent preventive treatment for pregnant women
IRS	Indoor residual spraying
ITN	Insecticide-treated mosquito net
LLIN	Long-lasting insecticide-treated mosquito net
LMHRA	Liberia Medicines and Health Products Regulatory Authority
LMIS	Logistics Management Information System
M&E	Monitoring and evaluation
MIP	Malaria in pregnancy
MIS	Malaria indicator survey
MOH	Ministry of Health
MOP	Malaria Operational Plan
NDS	National Drug Service
NDU	National Diagnostics Unit
NGO	Non-governmental organization
NMCP	National Malaria Control Program
NPHRL	National Public Health Reference Laboratory
OR	Operational research
PACS	Partnerships for Advancing Community-based Services
PMI	President's Malaria Initiative

QA/QC	Quality assurance/quality control
RBM	Roll Back Malaria
RDT	Rapid diagnostic test
SCMU	Supply Chain Management Unit
SP	Sulfadoxine-pyrimethamine
TA	Technical assistance
TTM	Trained traditional midwife
UNICEF	United Nations Children's Fund
USAID	United States Agency for International Development
USG	United States Government
WHO	World Health Organization

I. EXECUTIVE SUMMARY

When it was launched in 2005, the goal of the President's Malaria Initiative (PMI) was to reduce malaria-related mortality by 50% across 15 high-burden countries in sub-Saharan Africa through a rapid scale-up of four proven and highly effective malaria prevention and treatment measures: insecticide-treated mosquito nets (ITNs); indoor residual spraying (IRS); accurate diagnosis and prompt treatment with artemisinin-based combination therapies (ACTs); and intermittent preventive treatment for pregnant women (IPTp). With the passage of the Tom Lantos and Henry J. Hyde Global Leadership against HIV/AIDS, Tuberculosis, and Malaria Act in 2008, PMI developed a U.S. Government Malaria Strategy for 2009–2014. This strategy included a long-term vision for malaria control in which sustained high coverage with malaria prevention and treatment interventions would progressively lead to malaria-free zones in Africa, with the ultimate goal of worldwide malaria eradication by 2040-2050. Consistent with this strategy and the increase in annual appropriations supporting PMI, four new sub-Saharan African countries and one regional program in the Greater Mekong Subregion of Southeast Asia were added in 2011. The contributions of PMI, together with those of other partners, have led to dramatic improvements in the coverage of malaria control interventions in PMI-supported countries, and all 15 original countries have documented substantial declines in all-cause mortality rates among children less than five years of age.

In 2015, PMI launched the next six-year strategy, setting forth a bold and ambitious goal and objectives. This PMI Strategy 2015-2020 takes into account the progress over the past decade and the new challenges that have arisen. Malaria prevention and control remains a major U.S. foreign assistance objective and PMI's Strategy fully aligns with the U.S. Government's vision of ending preventable child and maternal deaths and ending extreme poverty. It is also in line with the goals articulated in the RBM Partnership's second generation global malaria action plan, *Action and Investment to defeat Malaria (AIM) 2016-2030: for a Malaria-Free World* and WHO's updated *Global Technical Strategy: 2016-2030*. Under the PMI Strategy for 2015-2020, the U.S. Government's goal is to work with PMI-supported countries and partners to further reduce malaria deaths and substantially decrease malaria morbidity, towards the long-term goal of elimination.

Liberia was selected as a PMI focus country in FY 2008.

This FY 2016 Malaria Operational Plan presents a detailed implementation plan for Liberia, based on the strategies of PMI and the National Malaria Control Program (NMCP). It was developed in consultation with the NMCP and with the participation of national and international partners involved in malaria prevention and control in the country. The activities that PMI is proposing to support fit in well with the National Malaria Control strategy and plan and build on investments made by PMI and other partners to improve and expand malaria-related services, including the Global Fund to Fight AIDS, Tuberculosis, and Malaria (Global Fund) malaria grants. This plan was developed just after the 2014/2015 Liberia Ebola epidemic subsided. The Ebola crisis brought about massive disruptions in public and private health service delivery, historic reductions in health system health seeking by the population at large, and Ebola-related deaths among the health sector workforce. Thus this plan was developed during a period characterized by intense government and donor health system restoration and recovery focused efforts in Liberia. This document briefly reviews the current status of malaria control policies and interventions in Liberia, describes progress to date, identifies challenges and unmet needs to achieving the targets of the NMCP and PMI, particularly challenges encountered over the previous year as a result of Ebola, and provides a description of activities that are planned with FY 2016 funding.

The proposed FY 2016 PMI budget for Liberia is $12 million. PMI will support the following intervention areas with these funds:

Insecticide-treated nets (ITNs): In its Strategic Plan and Operational Guidelines on Long-Lasting Insecticidal Nets, Liberia adopted a "universal coverage" goal for ITNs. Universal coverage was defined operationally as one long-lasting insecticide-treated mosquito net (LLIN) for each sleeping space, or a maximum of three LLINs per household. The country has set objectives of 90% of families receiving at least one LLIN, and at least 85% of the general population sleeping under LLINs. Currently, mass campaigns are the main distribution method, reinforced by intense behavior change communication at the community level. The NMCP also aims to complement campaigns with continuous distribution of nets during the first antenatal care (ANC) visit and at delivery in a registered health care institution. Between 2008 and 2014 nearly 4.6 million LLINs were distributed in Liberia through rolling campaigns, ANC services, and at institutional delivery, including approximately 1.7 million LLINs purchased by PMI. In 2015, approximately 2.8 million nets procured by the Global Fund were distributed throughout Liberia in the country's first nationwide mass campaign. PMI will support post-distribution activities for the recently completed 2015 national wide mass campaign, including a post-distribution campaign survey.

The planned activities with FY 2016 funding include procurement and distribution of 320,000 LLINs for routine distribution and technical support for Liberia's routine distribution channels. Furthermore, PMI will support planning for Liberia's next universal coverage mass campaign, which should take place in 2018.

Indoor residual spraying (IRS) and entomological monitoring: PMI supported IRS in Liberia from 2009 to 2013. The last time IRS was conducted, PMI supported spraying with a long-lasting organophosphate due to the observation of significant pyrethroid resistance throughout Liberia and the requirement to spray carbamates twice during the malaria transmission season because of their short residual life. However, because of the higher cost of the long-lasting organophosphate, only 10% of the Liberian population could be protected with IRS in 2013, compared with 23% of the population on a similar budget the previous year. Therefore, after consultations within the PMI interagency team and discussions with the NMCP, the decision was made to suspend PMI-supported IRS in Liberia, and instead focus on increased entomological monitoring and universal LLIN coverage. Over the past year PMI supported the NMCP to evaluate the spatial and temporal composition of anopheline mosquitoes at two sites through pyrethrum spray collections, human landing catches, and Centers for Disease Control and Prevention light traps. In addition, insecticide susceptibility testing was supported at sites in six counties in 2014, which will be repeated in 2015 along with sites in five additional counties.

With FY 2016 funding PMI will continue to assist the NMCP in setting up a comprehensive mosquito surveillance program. Specifically, PMI will work to characterize insecticide susceptibility in Liberia's five regions, determine the distribution of anopheline species, support a full-time entomologist to sit with the NMCP to help build capacity and support on-the-job training, and maintain and support a functional insectary.

Malaria in pregnancy (MIP): Liberia's policy on MIP is a three-pronged approach, which consists of prompt and effective case management of malaria and anemia, IPTp with more than two doses of SP and use of LLINs. According to the 2013 DHS, 48% of pregnant women received two or more doses of IPTp during their last pregnancy. During the past two years, PMI assisted the NMCP in finalizing and launching updated MIP protocols and treatment guidelines based on new recommendations released by WHO in 2012. These new guidelines were harmonized across all MIP and case management related documents, and the documents were revised for nationwide use. With FY 2016 funding, PMI will continue to provide technical assistance to support the NMCP in the implementation, scale-up, and monitoring of MIP, including implementation of the new IPTp guidelines. Specifically, PMI will maintain its support to practicum sites related to training institutions, capacity building of health providers, in-service training and supervision for health care workers, and technical assistance to strengthen the distribution of MIP commodities.

Case management:
The National Malaria Strategic Plan stresses parasitological diagnosis for all suspected malaria cases at both the facility and community level in Liberia. As of 2014, RDTs were provided to all public facilities and private facilities that provided clinical services and agreed to report via the Health Management Information System (HMIS). Progress was also being made in expansion to retail pharmacies and medicine shops in Montserrado County, and at the community level through integrated community case management (iCCM) with UNICEF in four counties (Maryland, River Gee, Sinoe, and Grand Geddeh). In 2014 the Ebola epidemic and emergency response called for a suspension of malaria diagnostic testing of febrile persons by non-medical personnel such as general community health volunteers (gCHVs) in community settings of iCCM, and by extension to retail pharmacies and medicine shops, and to health care facilities if adequate infection prevention control supplies and training were not available. PMI continues to work with the NMCP to plan for reintroduction of testing for suspected malaria cases at all levels of the health system. With FY 2016 funding, PMI will procure laboratory supplies, including reagents for microscopy and approximately 1.4 million rapid diagnostic tests (RDTs). PMI will also continue to support strengthening of the National Public Health Reference Laboratory and will support the NMCP's efforts to conduct refresher training for laboratory technicians.

In 2013, the HMIS reported administration of 1 million artemisinin-based combination therapy (ACT) treatments, which represents 81% of the estimated 1.48 million malaria cases reported that were either clinically diagnosed or positive by microscopy or RDT. These figures almost certainly represent only a portion of the projected need because they overlap with a temporary moratorium on procurement of diagnostic and case management commodities. In addition, the massive disruption to the health system that resulted from the 2014/2015 Ebola epidemic makes more recent consumption figures an even less reliable basis for quantification. With FY 2016 funding, PMI will continue to procure strategic supplies of ACTs (approximately 1 million ACT treatments) for public/private sector health care facilities and community case management. Artesunate and artemether for treatment of severe malaria will also be procured. In addition, PMI will continue to support the extension of malaria case management to the community level and refresher training for facility-level case management. PMI will also support the quality assurance of antimalarial products. PMI intends to use FY 2016 funding to expand the reach of its case management efforts through technical assistance beyond the central ministry and three United States Agency for International Development (USAID) focus counties (Bong, Lofa, and Nimba) to the remaining 12 counties.

In response to a temporary moratorium on United States Government- and Global Fund procured commodities between May and August 2013, and with coordinated support from PMI and the Global Fund, the MOH and National Drug Service worked to develop an "interim approach" to strengthen commodity distribution and improve internal controls using a "top-up" system whereby MOH staff accompany deliveries and verify stock reports from the county level down to the facility level. In 2014, the aforementioned system-wide suspension of diagnostic testing and massive disruption to the public and private sector health systems resulted in widespread underutilization. The MOH and partners are currently developing plans to either submit a concept note under the Global Fund's New Funding Model or alternatively submit a costed extension to the existing Round 10 grant. Either option will require a thorough quantification of anticipated needs for diagnostic and treatment commodities as well as a review of current pipelines to define the full gap in commodities and implementation needs. It is anticipated that Global Fund will support most of the malaria commodities needed in calendar year 2017, as PMI is better positioned to provide the technical support to plan and distribute them. With FY 2016 funds, PMI will continue to support strengthening of the drug and laboratory supply chain system at the central and county levels.

Health systems strengthening and capacity building: PMI supports a range of targeted health system strengthening activities that cut across intervention areas but bolster achievement of malaria program results, such as training of health workers, supply chain management and health information systems strengthening, drug quality monitoring, and NCMP capacity building. To encourage integration of malaria prevention and control activities into routine health care in ways that are sustainable, PMI has supported the NMCP to more actively engage with other parts of the MOH involved in malaria-related activities.

A high priority of the NMCP is to increase the qualifications of its staff, particularly in terms of their managerial and supervisory capacity. Liberia has had a favorable experience with long-term technical assistance recently inaugurated through PMI for assistance with implementation Global Fund activities; therefore, with FY 2016 funding PMI will support two technical assistance positions in order to sustain and further improvements to the NMCP's management and oversight, both internally and externally. In addition, PMI will provide support to the central MOH/NMCP and community health teams to strengthen crosscutting health systems functions to improve management and governance of the health system, and support decentralization. PMI will also collaborate closely across United States Government agencies involved in post Ebola health system recovery efforts to leverage health system infrastructure and capacity building investments where possible.

Behavior change communication (BCC): The current BCC strategy focuses on the dissemination of malaria-related messaging through mass media, interpersonal communication and community engagement activities to help ensure that children under five years of age receive a diagnostic test and, if positive, effective ACT treatment within 24 hours, that pregnant women receive IPTp at every ANC visit after the first trimester, and that community members are aware of the benefits of and are using LLINs to prevent malaria. Over the past year, PMI continued to assist the MOH in developing communication materials, as well as training and equipping health providers, including gCHVs, to convey malaria messages. With FY 2016 funds, PMI will support the continued implementation of integrated interpersonal communication, including health provider training in Bong, Lofa, Nimba, Margibi, and Montserrado counties and will support BCC through community health services interventions/interpersonal communication, and mass media communications throughout the country.

Monitoring and evaluation (M&E): The NMCP has an M&E strategy and a costed M&E work plan. The Global Fund and PMI provide the bulk of the funding for M&E activities, while WHO provides technical support. The MOH has a fully integrated computerized HMIS that serves all public facilities and those private clinical facilities that receive malaria medications and diagnostic support from the MOH. Personnel have been trained and the system is operational nationwide; however, reporting is not uniform and data are underutilized at all levels, primarily summarized for monthly reports to the next level and not used to track trends in malaria cases. With FY 2016 funds, PMI will support continued implementation of the end-use verification survey of the availability of malaria commodities and the quality of services at the health facility level. PMI will also provide resources for supportive supervision of M&E activities from the national level, and for malaria data collection and use at the county level across all counties. Additionally, FY 2016 funds will be used to support therapeutic efficacy monitoring in 2017 and the 2019 Demographic Health Survey.

Operational research (OR): The NMCP Research, Monitoring, and Evaluation Department is responsible for planning and conducting operational research studies in collaboration with other NMCP focal points and partners. Liberia had one PMI-supported OR study that was completed in 2013, which examined using a dried blood tube sample as a stable source of quality control samples for RDTs in an external quality assurance system in the field. Liberia does not have any ongoing studies or studies planned with FY 2016 funding.

II. STRATEGY

1. Introduction

When it was launched in 2005, the goal of PMI was to reduce malaria-related mortality by 50% across 15 high-burden countries in sub-Saharan Africa through a rapid scale-up of four proven and highly effective malaria prevention and treatment measures: insecticide-treated mosquito nets (ITNs); indoor residual spraying (IRS); accurate diagnosis and prompt treatment with artemisinin-based combination therapies (ACTs); and intermittent preventive treatment for pregnant women (IPTp). With the passage of the Tom Lantos and Henry J. Hyde Global Leadership against HIV/AIDS, Tuberculosis, and Malaria Act in 2008, PMI developed a U.S. Government Malaria Strategy for 2009–2014. This strategy included a long-term vision for malaria control in which sustained high coverage with malaria prevention and treatment interventions would progressively lead to malaria-free zones in Africa, with the ultimate goal of worldwide malaria eradication by 2040-2050. Consistent with this strategy and the increase in annual appropriations supporting PMI, four new sub-Saharan African countries and one regional program in the Greater Mekong Subregion of Southeast Asia were added in 2011. The contributions of PMI, together with those of other partners, have led to dramatic improvements in the coverage of malaria control interventions in PMI-supported countries, and all 15 original countries have documented substantial declines in all-cause mortality rates among children less than five years of age.

In 2015, PMI launched the next six-year strategy, setting forth a bold and ambitious goal and objectives. This PMI Strategy for 2015-2020 takes into account the progress over the past decade and the new challenges that have arisen. Malaria prevention and control remains a major U.S. foreign assistance objective and PMI's Strategy fully aligns with the U.S. Government's vision of ending preventable child and maternal deaths and ending extreme poverty. It is also in line with the goals articulated in the RBM Partnership's second generation global malaria action plan, *Action and Investment to defeat Malaria (AIM) 2016-2030: for a Malaria-Free World* and WHO's updated *Global Technical Strategy: 2016-2030*. Under the PMI Strategy 2015-2020, the U.S. Government's goal is to work with PMI-supported countries and partners to further reduce malaria deaths and substantially decrease malaria morbidity, towards the long-term goal of elimination.

Liberia was selected as a PMI focus country in FY 2008.

This FY 2016 Malaria Operational Plan presents a detailed implementation plan for Liberia, based on the investments and strategic approach of PMI to date and the National Malaria Control Program (NMCP) strategy. It was developed in consultation with the NMCP and with the participation of national and international partners involved in malaria prevention and control in the country. The activities that PMI is proposing to support fit in well with the National Malaria Control strategy and plan and build on investments made by PMI and other partners to improve and expand malaria-related services, including the Global Fund to Fight AIDS, Tuberculosis, and Malaria (Global Fund) malaria grants. This plan was developed just after the 2014/2015 Liberia Ebola epidemic subsided. The Ebola crisis brought about massive disruptions in public and private health service delivery, historic reductions in health system health seeking by the population at large, and Ebola-related deaths among the health sector workforce. Thus this plan was developed during a period characterized by intense government and donor health system restoration and recovery focused efforts in Liberia. This document briefly reviews the current status of malaria control policies and interventions in Liberia, describes progress to date, particularly challenges encountered over the previous year as a result of Ebola, identifies challenges and unmet needs to achieving the targets of the NMCP and PMI, and provides a description of activities that are planned with FY 2016 funding.

2. Malaria situation in Liberia

Liberia covers 43,000 square miles in West Africa, and it is bounded by nearly 350 miles of Atlantic Ocean off the southwest and by the neighboring countries of Sierra Leone (northwest), Guinea (north), and Côte d'Ivoire (east and southeast). Most of the country lies at altitudes below 500 meters. The coastal areas are characterized by mangrove swamps, which give way to tropical rain forest that gradually thins out northwards to be replaced by deciduous forest. All geographic areas of Liberia are favorable to malaria transmission. Liberia has hyper-/holoendemic malaria. The major vectors for malaria are *Anopheles gambiae* s.s., *An. funestus*, and *An. melas*. The major parasite species are *Plasmodium falciparum* (>90%), *P. ovale*, and *P. malariae*.[1]

According to results from the 2005 Malaria Indicator Survey (MIS), the prevalence of malaria parasitemia in children under five by RDT was 66%. The prevalence rate as measured by microscopy was 32% in 2009, and was 28% according to the 2011 MIS. The geographical prevalence of malaria according to the 2011 MIS is shown in the map below.

Prevalence of Malaria Parasitemia in Children under Five Years of Age by Region, Liberia 2011 MIS

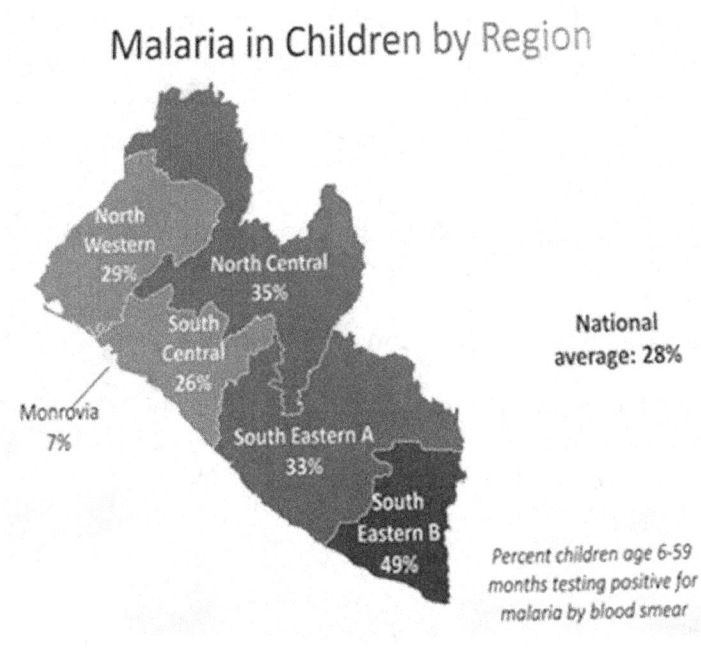

---

[1] Roll Back Malaria-National Desk Analysis-Liberia- 2001

The entire population of approximately 4 million[2] is at risk of the disease; children under five and pregnant women are the most affected groups. According to reports received by the World Health Organization (WHO) in 2010 from the NMCP, approximately 40% of consultations in outpatient departments in all age groups in public health facilities were due to malaria.[3] The 2009 Health Facility Survey (HFS) estimated that malaria accounts for 33% of in-patient deaths.

Since August 2005, Liberia has made considerable progress in malaria control and prevention. The achievements from August 2005 to 2013 documented in the 2013 Demographic and Health Survey (DHS) are included in the section on coverage/impact indicators to date.

However it must be noted that the extent of the impact of the 2014/2015 Ebola crisis on progress achieved to date in malaria control in Liberia noted above is not yet known. Massive disruptions in health service delivery and distrust in the health system by the population were well-documented. Data suggesting significant setbacks in progress include: coverage of IPTp for prevention of malaria in pregnancy dropped from 52% in April 2014 to 15.5% in August 2014 and 9.5% in November 2014; and the average monthly number of malaria cases treated with ACTs in the public sector dropped by more than 52% during the September-December 2014 period, when compared with the 7 months prior.

3. **Country health system delivery structure and Ministry of Health (MOH) organization**

The health system in Liberia is set up in a pyramid structure with community health volunteers as the foundation. Community health volunteers include household health promoters, trained traditional midwives (TTMs), and general community health volunteers (gCHVs). Together, these groups serve outreach functions with prevention messaging and referrals to health clinics and health centers. In some areas, gCHVs also participate in directly observed treatment for tuberculosis and integrated community case management (iCCM) for diarrhea, acute respiratory infections, and malaria.

Health clinics are the primary care unit of the health system and are meant to have at least two professional staff: a nurse and a certified midwife.[4] With catchment areas 10 km in diameter, clinics typically serve populations of 3,500 – 12,000 and are mandated to be open eight hours a day, five days a week. Clinics are intended for outpatient care, and their beds are for observation only. Patients requiring further supervised care are referred to health centers or hospitals.

Health centers provide larger catchment populations of around 25,000 – 40,000 with secondary care, focusing on maternal and child health care. These centers are open 24 hours a day, every day and are meant to have up to 40 beds, laboratory diagnostic services, and provide services for severe medical and obstetric care.

---

[2] 2015 estimate; National Population and Housing Census, 2008 plus a growth rate of 2.1%
[3] http://www.aho.afro.who.int/profiles_information/index.php/File:Reported_malaria_cases_by_county.PNG
[4] Due to the shortage of certified midwives, this combination also takes the shape of a licensed practical nurse and TTM

Cases requiring surgical intervention are referred to hospitals, which are meant to be equipped with an operating theater, advanced laboratory, basic radiography, and basic ultrasonography. In addition to secondary care, hospitals have outpatient departments, which provide surrounding residents with primary care.

The MOH is working to decentralize responsibility for service delivery from the central ministry to the county level, and this mandate includes delegating responsibility, authority, and resources to the counties, so they can effectively manage the systems that most significantly affect the day-to-day delivery of health care. For the last five years, the MOH has contracted out most of the service delivery to non-governmental organizations (NGOs) with donor funding, focusing on stewardship functions and management tasks, but Liberia is seeing a shift towards placing more responsibility on the county health teams (CHTs) to directly manage local health systems and oversee service delivery. The United States Agency for International Development (USAID)/Liberia is committed to the MOH strategy and is focused on improving the capacity of CHTs to effectively make this transition.

4. National malaria control strategy

The Government of Liberia (GOL)/MOH's Liberian Malaria Control Strategy for 2010-2015 aims to sustain progress in reducing malaria-related mortality, scale-up the most effective malaria control and prevention activities from the health facility to the community level, and involve all partners (including the private sector) in supporting health care delivery. A new five-year strategy through 2020 was developed following a Malaria Program Review in 2014, has been validated, and is currently being costed.

Under the 2010-2015 Liberia Malaria Control Strategy, the NMCP assumes the lead coordination role and takes responsibility for the decentralization of malaria control and prevention activities throughout the country by gradually devolving implementation responsibilities to CHTs. This coordination role includes all health partners, donors, and private sector stakeholders.

Malaria control and prevention activities in Liberia follow the principle of the "three ones":

- One national malaria control coordinating authority where implementation is a country-led process
- One comprehensive plan for malaria control, including costed work plans
- One country-level monitoring and evaluation framework

The four basic technical pillars or strategic interventions are:

1. *Case management through improved malaria treatment and the scale-up of ACTs*. Resources are to be directed towards increasing the availability and use of malaria diagnostic tools and ACTs as first-line treatment in all public health facilities, at the community level, and in the private sector. To ensure quality of care, training will focus on strengthening key providers' skills. Malaria treatment guidelines will be revised to ensure coordinated implementation at all levels. National targets include:

- At least 80% of patients with uncomplicated malaria receive early diagnosis and prompt and effective treatment according to MOH guidelines
- At least 65% of patients with complicated or severe malaria are diagnosed in a timely manner and receive correct treatment according to MOH guidelines

2. Integrated vector management to prevent mosquito-to-human contact, to reduce vector abundance, and to improve environmental sanitation and control of potential breeding sites. Integrated vector management in Liberia includes the provision of long-lasting insecticide-treated nets (LLINs) through mass distribution to all households and targeted distribution to pregnant women and children under five. Although the strategy also includes targeted indoor residual spraying (IRS) for sleeping structures and targeted larviciding, the NMCP does not currently have support for IRS or larviciding activities. In its Strategic Plan and Operational Guidelines on Long-Lasting Insecticidal Nets for Liberia 2012-2017, Liberia adopted a "universal coverage" goal for ITNs, defined operationally as one LLIN for each sleeping space or a maximum of three LLINs per household.

National targets include:

- At least 90% of families have received at least one LLIN
- At least 85% of children and pregnant women sleep under LLINs
- At least 85% of the general population sleeps under LLINs
- At least 85% of the population in targeted districts is protected by IRS

3. Malaria prevention and control during pregnancy. Since the introduction of intermittent preventive treatment for pregnant women (IPTp) in Liberia in 2004, the use of sulfadoxine-pyrimethamine (SP) for malaria prevention during pregnancy has been gradually increasing, paralleling the gradual increase in access to health care. Trained traditional midwives are expected to refer pregnant women to ANC clinics rather than supply IPTp at the community level. However, for pregnant women residing more than five kilometers from ANC services, certified midwives deliver ANC services, including SP, while also encouraging early and repeated ANC clinic attendance. National targets include:

- At least 80% of pregnant women attending antenatal consultation receive IPTp2 according to the national MIP protocol
- 80% of all pregnant women diagnosed with malaria at health facilities (public or private) receive prompt and effective treatment according to national treatment protocol
- All pregnant women with suspected malaria at the community level are referred to the nearest health facility and receive prompt and effective treatment
- At least 80% of pregnant women attending antenatal consultation receive an LLIN

4. *Support for advocacy, social mobilization, and behavior change communication (BCC).* This component will focus on the role of health providers and the community in malaria control and prevention activities, using a multichannel approach for health education with emphasis on radio messages, community health volunteers, and child-to-child communication. Key change agents for dissemination of malaria messages will include peer educators, trained caregivers, and other locally respected authorities. National targets include:

- All health facilities (public and private) provide updated malaria health education
- 90% of the population has heard a malaria message through multimedia channels

The above four technical pillars in turn rest on a foundation of support functions designed to facilitate their effective rollout and implementation in a cross-cutting manner.

- **M&E and Research**: Monitoring and evaluation is a major focus of both the MOH and the NMCP. The NMCP has developed a comprehensive M&E plan in collaboration with the M&E unit of the Department of Planning at the MOH and with other technical partners. This plan will be integrated with the health management and information system (HMIS) of the MOH. More detailed operational M&E plans will be prepared on an annual basis and revised when necessary. Malaria-specific indicators will be selected from the RBM core indicators, as well as program-specific indicators to measure performance. All data collected (routine and surveys) will be analyzed, and reports will be produced and shared with stakeholders.
- **Supply Chain Management**: Supply chain management continues to be one of the biggest challenges facing health care programs in Liberia. Inadequate storage, inventory and warehouse management practices, and limited information sharing continue to contribute to stockouts of commodities and uncertain drug quality. The NMCP and the public health community see this activity as a key priority.
- **Program Management and Administration**: In order to ensure that the NMCP is able to provide expert advice on malaria prevention and control activities in Liberia, additional capacity building, particularly in program management and M&E are required. This capacity building will be a continuous process that will provide the NMCP with the technical capabilities, resources, and information needed to carry out its responsibilities, including fostering effective partnerships among stakeholders.

5. Updates in the strategy section

Ebola Virus Disease Outbreak

Before the 2014 start of the Ebola epidemic, Liberia was considered to be one of the poorest countries in the world, ranking 175 of 187 on the UNDP Human Development Index (2013). The country was still rebuilding after a civil war through much of the 1990s, which ended in 2003, and was making substantial progress in improving the health status of its citizens until the onset of the Ebola epidemic. The first report confirming Ebola virus disease (EVD) in Guinea with suspicious deaths in Liberia that were under investigation was March 24, 2014. The epidemic peaked in mid-September 2014, with another slightly smaller peak in December 2014.

As a result of the Ebola epidemic, Liberia experienced dramatic declines in public health indicators and in the delivery of basic health care, reversing years of progress in improving the health of Liberians, particularly women and children. For example, measles vaccination rates dropped from 77.8% in January 2014 to 44.8% in January 2015. During this same time frame, health facility deliveries declined from 65% to 27.8%, deliveries attended by skilled providers dropped from 61% to 30.6% and pregnant women having the recommended four or more antenatal care visits declined from 78.1% to 31.3%.[5]

Basic primary health care services virtually stopped functioning in a climate of little or no confidence in the safety of the health system, on the part of both service providers and clients. This was caused by deep fear among providers coupled with a lack of adequate training and personal protective equipment to deliver services safely, and in some cases reassignment of health workers to Ebola Treatment Units. Community-based health services, still at a nascent stage before the crisis, also broke down. In many locations, general community health volunteers (gCHVs) with limited training and few supplies served as the only health service available, apart from private drug-sellers and "pharmacies." Many large health centers and hospitals, already struggling before the Ebola outbreak, were similarly unprepared to diagnose or manage suspected Ebola cases and were quickly overwhelmed, leading to nosocomial Ebola infections, declines in other services, and fear of the health care system.

Those facilities that remained open provided only rapid identification and triage of suspected Ebola patients; some turned away patients altogether. Many settings, lacking adequate infection prevention control training and personal protective equipment, moved to a "no-touch" approach of treating major causes of morbidity and mortality in order to reduce the risk to health workers. Specifically with respect to malaria, despite great progress made in scaling up diagnosis for malaria prior to the Ebola crisis, parasitologic diagnosis was suspended. Outpatient visits dropped 61% nationwide between August and October 2014. And recorded malaria cases plummeted, yet with the WHO and other experts suspecting a likely increase in actual malaria cases among the population as a result of the crisis.

During the first quarter of 2015, rapid progress was made on reopening facilities, though full restoration of services remains a work in progress. By January 8, the MOH was reporting that 100% of public facilities were "open," although only 52% had established triage systems to quickly identify people at risk for Ebola. There was little reliable data about the extent of services being provided. On May 9, WHO announced the end of the Ebola outbreak in Liberia; however, on June 29, 2015, a confirmed case of Ebola was reported in Liberia and five contacts associated with that case were confirmed to have Ebola. All contacts have now completed their 21-day monitoring period and the country was declared Ebola free for the second time on September 3, 2015. As the focus on Ebola response has waned, the GOL has shifted its attention to recovery efforts and the United States Government (USG) country team has been working to address urgent short term health needs such as malaria; plan for longer term investments that will

---

[5] UNICEF 2014 (based on analysis of Liberia HMIS 2014 as of October 2014)

shore up health worker capacity, strengthen critical components of the health system, and prepare to address future epidemics. As of May 2015, the USG, United Nations partners, and private NGOs and donors were supporting facility reopening and training and supervision of staff, distributing personal protective equipment, and restoring community-based services, including malaria services.

Lessons learned from the Ebola epidemic in regard to PMI and malaria control in general:

1. PMI-supported projects were well positioned to assist with the Ebola response. For example, support for strengthening the HMIS allowed Liberia to monitor the situation via the HMIS, whereas Guinea had to rely on their integrated disease surveillance and response system. In addition, PMI support for service delivery allowed a platform for introduction of infection prevention and control. Furthermore, PMI support for the National Drug Stores (NDS) and supply chain activities meant personnel were in place to consult on inventory control and supply chain issues pertaining to delivery of infection prevention and control commodities.

2. Already existing relationships through PMI led to:
   a. Quick and effective actions on the part of both CDC and USAID with the MOH in terms of cooperation and support.
   b. Early and sustained coordination with NGO partners in support of the NMCP and the MOH, particularly the "no touch" policy for malaria management.
   c. Recognition of the emotional element and stresses on Liberian colleagues that could never be appreciated long distance or over the phone and being able to adjust the tenor of the dialogue to be supportive of, in essence, a grieving process.
   d. Flexibility. As soon as discussions regarding "no touch" and presumptive treatment began, PMI was able to scrutinize stock levels and scheduled deliveries of commodities already ordered and pending. As a result, the number of planned RDTs was halved and the numbers of antimalarials were increased.
   e. Adaptability. As the EVD crisis heightened and health facilities closed leading to a drop off in HMIS reporting, other data sets, such as the data from a private sector ACT pilot project, became important. Training and close supervision by the NGO for adherence to triage and infection control allowed the private sector outlets to continue to function when most of the surrounding health facilities closed, and the data reflected a corresponding upsurge in utilization of the medicine stores and pharmacies.
   f. Creativity. PMI and the NMCP worked with *Médecins Sans Frontières* to advise on mass drug administration (e.g., regarding local sensitivities and collateral effects, such as the need to inform local dispensers and help them devise questions to determine if a client had consumed freely distributed ACTs prior to the consultation). An evaluation conducted after the first round of mass drug administration provided essential feedback (e.g., messaging on when to take medication and issues with hoarding) in time for the second round of administration in Liberia and subsequent plans in Sierra Leone.

3. There have been several benefits to malaria control from the Ebola response. These include:

   a. A specimen transport system developed for EVD, but also designed to accommodate malaria slides, providing a potential opportunity to route quality assurance specimens.
   b. Community empowerment, which played a key role in the response to EVD is now being used by the NMCP, PMI, and partners as a model to pilot changing social norms regarding net use and IPTp.
   c. Enhanced data management skills for analysis and utilization of data for local decision-making through training of national and county health staff.
   d. Enhanced emphasis on surveillance, particularly reporting of deaths.

Government of Liberia Health Sector Plans

As part of its overall Ebola recovery efforts, the GOL has developed an integrated Investment Plan for Building a Resilient Health System (2015-2021) with a particular focus on the restoration of essential primary health care services as part of the development of a more resilient health system post-Ebola. The three overarching objectives of the plan are to promote universal access to safe, quality services under Liberia's Essential Package of Health Services; strengthen capacity to prevent, detect, and respond to infectious disease threats; and restore trust in the health system. The plan calls for investment in the health workforce, health infrastructure, and epidemic preparedness. It also envisions improved supply chains; better infection prevention and control; more comprehensive health information and surveillance systems; sustained community engagement; and strengthened capacity for leadership, governance, and health financing.

6. Integration, collaboration, and coordination

The Global Health Initiative (GHI) is the USG vehicle for ensuring all USG global health investments are efficiently coordinated with recipient countries' health priorities in order to achieve maximum ownership and results. Thus, the guiding principle of the USG's GHI strategy for Liberia is to ensure all USG health investments align with Liberia's 2011-2021 National Health and Social Welfare Policy and Plan, which is designed to expand access to basic health services and to establish the building blocks of equitable, effective, responsive, and sustainable health service delivery. The USG complements the Liberian MOH's efforts by concentrating its resources on two key focus areas: 1) improving service delivery through the Essential Package of Health Services and 2) strengthening health systems to increase institutional capacity and sustainability.

Through GHI, the USG will invest in capacity building and technical assistance for policy formulation, strategy development, health systems strengthening, and countrywide BCC initiatives. Additionally, the USG is using MOH systems to provide both facility-based and community-based support under performance-based contracting with NGOs for specific health facilities and their catchment communities. The USG is also providing complementary technical assistance for quality assurance, in-service training, and supportive supervision.

Performance-based contracting is a service agreement entered into between the MOH and NGOs to carry out service delivery at health facilities and catchment communities. These NGOs are expected to ensure health care services are in accordance with the Essential Package of Health Services, which is a standard government-approved package for primary health care services in Liberia. These contracts include a performance bonus for reaching targets on quantity and quality indicators after verification of submitted data at the county level and counter-verification by the central level committee comprised of the MOH and third party stakeholders.

From 2005 until 2007, the Global Fund constituted the majority of external funding for the implementation of malaria control and prevention activities in Liberia. A $37 million Global Fund Round 7 grant was signed in April 2008, with the United Nations Development Program as the Principal Recipient, and in 2011 a $60 million Round 10 grant was signed with the MOH and an NGO, Plan Liberia, as the two Principal Recipients. Based on the Phase 1 evaluation of the Round 10 grant that was completed in 2013 and Liberia's approved Phase 2 award signed in April 2014, the funding available for Round 10 was approximately $35 million for the period through June 2016. However, planned implementation of some Global Fund grant activities stalled as a result of the Ebola crisis. The MOH is currently in dialogue with the Global Fund about the country's decision of whether to request a costed extension of the Round 10 grant with inclusion of the New Funding Model $4 million malaria allocation or to prepare a full concept note under the New Funding Model based on an updated National Malaria Strategic Plan and country dialogue covering the period from July 2016 through December 2017.

As PMI complements the activities under the Global Fund, support was provided to the NMCP and other parties during the evaluation of the first phase and during the development of the proposal for the second phase of the Round 10 grant, which is now in operation. PMI provided technical assistance, particularly regarding the quantification of commodities. A key element supported by the Global Fund Round 10 grant involved a national mass distribution of LLINs. This was a change from the previous strategy of rolling mass distribution of LLINs, during which different parts of the country received nets at different times. The LLIN campaign, originally planned for 2014, was delayed due to the need to reconfigure to an emergency distribution plan in the setting of Ebola control efforts and minimizing individual contact for worker and community safety. Going forward, in coordination with the NMCP, it was agreed that the Global Fund would provide the LLINs for nationwide campaigns and that PMI would provide LLINs for routine distribution through ANC visits and at delivery in a health care institution and technical assistance for both types of distribution.

Liberia underwent a Malaria Program Review with an *Aide Mémoire* outlining the findings and recommendations signed in March 2014 by the MOH, USAID, Plan Liberia as the Global Fund co-Principal Recipient with the MOH, and WHO. This review effort has informed the process of updating Liberia's National Malaria Strategic Plan for the period 2016-2020.

In Liberia, PMI prioritizes the scale-up of iCCM to increase access to health services at the community level, and in collaboration with UNICEF and other partners, PMI supports the Community Health Services Division of the MOH to implement iCCM. This program provides diagnosis and treatment for malaria, diarrhea, and acute respiratory infections for children under five at the community level. The Global Fund, under its Round 10 grant, has committed support to the expansion of the iCCM program from 2% to 5% of the number of national febrile episodes tested for malaria and treated if positive. Although iCCM activities were impacted by the Ebola crisis, the NMCP has renewed its focus for supporting the nationwide implementation of iCCM in collaboration with PMI and other partners.

The MOH has prioritized the integration of diagnostic capacity for malaria, tuberculosis, and HIV at all levels. The MOH established a National Diagnostics Unit (NDU) to coordinate the support of partners to maintain achievements and continue progress. PMI and other USAID programs are coordinating with the NDU, the Global Fund, and other partners to operationalize an integrated diagnostics strategy that will provide comprehensive diagnostic policies, standard operational guidelines, and a national diagnostic program for Liberia. As part of the post Ebola health system recovery and rebuilding efforts, the U.S. government is working with the Government of Liberia and other international partners to transition laboratory capacity provided during the Ebola epidemic and strengthen Liberia's laboratory system over the long-term, including aspects that will benefit malaria diagnostics.

The MENTOR Initiative supported a pilot in the greater Monrovia area of Montserrado County to provide ACTs to private pharmacies and medicine shops for increased access to malaria treatment. This pilot provided testing with RDTs and treatment (if RDT-positive) to an estimated 0.5% of the national febrile cases. PMI has provided technical input to the NMCP, and based on results and lessons learned, the Global Fund will support the scale-up of this pilot private sector activity through their Round 10 Phase 2 grant to cover 3% of the projected national febrile cases annually, which represents 75% of the private sector pharmacies and medicine shops in Montserrado where the bulk of such facilities are found. In a rapid survey conducted by the MENTOR Initiative in May 2015 in Monrovia as part of their private sector pilot, over 50% of people reported going to a medicine store/pharmacy first for fever, whether for an adult or child, and according to the 2013 DHS, treatment seeking for children under five with a fever was 51.8% from the public sector, 36.5% from the private sector and 14.5% from another source. USAID's Office of Foreign Disaster Assistance built on MENTOR's work to expand its reach to additional private pharmacies during the Ebola outbreak to ensure malaria services remained available and were provided safely, and that pharmacy staff were trained on identification and referral of potential Ebola cases.

Additionally, PMI, in collaboration with the NMCP, had initiated a partnership with private companies to support implementation of IRS in the years that IRS was conducted. Under this initiative, the Arcelor Mittal Steel Company conducted three rounds of spraying in its concession areas in Nimba and Grand Bassa counties from 2010 to 2012. The Liberia Agriculture Company was also engaged in this public-private partnership and supported one round of spraying in its concessional area in Grand Bassa County in 2011. PMI provided insecticides and technical support, including training and mentoring, to these companies to build capacity to conduct IRS. As IRS has not been prioritized for MOP funding since FY 2013, the IRS equipment remains in storage, and the NMCP hopes to work in the future with these companies and other private sector sources to support IRS for their populations. PMI will continue to strengthen the vector control and entomological capacity of the NMCP to better understand vector ecology and insecticide resistance in collaboration with the U.S. Naval Medical Research Unit No. 3, the Liberian Institute for Biomedical Research, the Armed Forces of Liberia, and other groups such as the MENTOR Initiative who are collecting relevant data related to their individual projects.

7. PMI goal, objectives, strategic areas, and key indicators

Under the PMI Strategy for 2015-2020, the U.S. Government's goal is to work with PMI-supported countries and partners to further reduce malaria deaths and substantially decrease malaria morbidity, towards the long-term goal of elimination. Building upon the progress to date in PMI-supported countries, PMI will work with NMCPs and partners to accomplish the following objectives by 2020:

1. Reduce malaria mortality by one-third from 2015 levels in PMI-supported countries, achieving a greater than 80% reduction from PMI's original 2000 baseline levels.

2. Reduce malaria morbidity in PMI-supported countries by 40% from 2015 levels.

3. Assist at least five PMI-supported countries to meet the World Health Organization's (WHO) criteria for national or sub-national pre-elimination.[6]

These objectives will be accomplished by emphasizing five core areas of strategic focus:
1. Achieving and sustaining scale of proven interventions
2. Adapting to changing epidemiology and incorporating new tools
3. Improving countries' capacity to collect and use information
4. Mitigating risk against the current malaria control gains
5. Building capacity and health systems towards full country ownership

To track progress toward achieving and sustaining scale of proven interventions (area of strategic focus #1), PMI will continue to track the key indicators recommended by the Roll Back Malaria Monitoring and Evaluation Reference Group (RBM MERG) as listed below:

- Proportion of households with at least one ITN
- Proportion of households with at least one ITN for every two people
- Proportion of children under five years old who slept under an ITN the previous night
- Proportion of pregnant women who slept under an ITN the previous night
- Proportion of households in targeted districts protected by IRS
- Proportion of children under five years old with fever in the last two weeks for whom advice or treatment was sought
- Proportion of children under five with fever in the last two weeks who had a finger or heel stick
- Proportion receiving an ACT among children under five years old with fever in the last two weeks who received any antimalarial drugs
- Proportion of women who received two or more doses of IPTp for malaria during ANC visits during their last pregnancy

---

[6] http://whqlibdoc.who.int/publications/2007/9789241596084_eng.pdf

8. Progress on coverage/impact indicators to date

Table 1: Evolution of Key Malaria Indicators in Liberia from 2005 to 2013

Indicator	MIS 2005	DHS 2007	MIS 2009	MIS 2011	DHS 2013
% Households with at least one ITN	18%	30%[a]	47%	50%	55%
% Households with at least one ITN for every two people	n/a	n/a	n/a	17%	22%
% Children under five who slept under an ITN the previous night	3%	n/a	26%	37%	38%
% Pregnant women who slept under an ITN the previous night	n/a	n/a	33%	39%	37%
% Households in targeted districts protected by IRS	n/a	n/a	n/a	9%[b]	11%[b]
% Children under five years old with fever in the last two weeks for whom advice or treatment was sought	n/a	n/a	n/a	60%	71%
% Children under five with fever in the last two weeks who had a finger or heel stick	n/a	n/a	23%	33%	42%
% Children receiving an ACT among children under five years old with fever in the last two weeks who received any antimalarial drugs	n/a	n/a	45%	70%	43%[d]
% Women who received two or more doses of IPTp during their last pregnancy in the last two years	4%	12%[c]	45%	50%	48%

[a] The 2007 DHS only asked about any net ownership, not specifically about ITNs, and did not ask about net use
[b] This is out of all households
[c] The 2007 DHS only asked about pregnant women who took any SP
[d] There is a note in the 2013 DHS regarding some confusion on this question as an additional 42.2% (compared to only 9.9 % in 2011 MIS) reported use of amodiquine, which is how ASAQ is known in Liberia, making it difficult to distinguish between actual use of the mono vs. combination therapy.

9. Other relevant evidence on progress

The 2009 Health Facility Survey (HFS) also provides useful information on the progress of facility-based malaria activities. A total of 418 health facilities, representing 79% of all health facilities in Liberia, were visited, and the survey included record review, assessment of commodities, and observation of malaria case management. Results from the 2009 HFS were encouraging, as 86% of health workers were prescribing antimalarial drugs according to national guidelines and 85% of health workers had access to essential malaria drugs.

A follow-up HFS was undertaken in 2013, and as of August 2015 the report is still being finalized. The protocol and methodology of the 2009 survey was slightly different from the 2013 survey due to budget and other issues. For instance, the number of interviews was reduced for some forms per facility level (i.e., clinic, health center, and hospital). The initial review of the 2013 HFS report revealed some systematic issues with how the 2013 and previous data had been analyzed, and an effort was made to correct the 2013 report.

Table 2: Key Indicators of the Liberia Health Facility Surveys

	INDICATORS	HFS 2005*	HFS 2009
1	% of GOL health facilities that have all four presentation of ACTs available for treatment of uncomplicated malaria on the day of visit	58	71
2	% of health workers who search for danger signs	11	20
3	% of health workers who prescribe antimalarial drug according to national guidelines	75	86
4	% of health workers who counsel patients/caretakers on malaria	26	45
5	% of health workers with access to essential malaria drugs	48	85
6	% of out-patient department attendance due to malaria among children under five years	59**	38
7	% of pregnant women with confirmed malaria	31	18
8	% of patients receiving appropriate malaria treatment within 24 hours	21	35
9	% of overall deaths with laboratory-confirmed malaria (rapid diagnostic test or blood smear)	44	33

*The 2005 HFS was part of the 2005 MIS, which collected information from households and health facilities
**Clinical malaria

10. Challenges and opportunities

Although appreciable progress has been made, significant strides are required to further reduce malaria-related morbidity and mortality in Liberia, and at the present time to regain the gains lost during the Ebola crisis as mentioned previously. The main challenges remain the same and include: 1) inefficient supply chain management; 2) inadequate Logistics Management Information System (LMIS) reporting and use; and 3) need for greater capacity at the NMCP for managerial and supervisory functions. Pyrethroid resistance in Liberia is also a concern and a potential threat to the efficacy of ITNs. Significant pyrethroid resistance has been observed throughout Liberia (deltamethrin mortality rates from 2014 ranged from only 15-78%); however, the potential operational impact of the observed pyrethroid resistance is still unknown. The NMCP's 2010-2015 strategy included increased use of IRS, which could mitigate the threat of resistance, but under current budget constraints, restarting the IRS program in Liberia is not feasible. The current focus in Liberia is on improving and maintaining ITN access, as even in areas of pyrethroid resistance, LLINs act as a physical barrier and the irritancy of pyrethroids on the nets may still reduce mosquito blood-feeding.

Since its inception in 2008, PMI has allocated an average 40% of its annual budget to the procurement and distribution of antimalarial commodities. The supply chain for these commodities, particularly for ACTs and RDTs, is critical for diagnosis and treatment of malaria. Following reports of leakages and an ongoing lack of controls and safeguards to ensure secure delivery of USG-procured commodities, the USG together with the Global Fund issued a temporary moratorium between May and August 2013 on the disbursement of USG-procured malaria and reproductive health commodities, and Global Fund-procured malaria commodities. In response, and with coordinated support from PMI and the Global Fund, the MOH and National Drug Service (NDS) worked to develop an "interim approach" to strengthen commodity distribution and improve internal controls using a "top-up" system whereby MOH staff accompany deliveries and verify stock reports from the county level down to the facility level. The interim approach is designed to ensure that re-supply is based on collected data, which is verified and validated through an approval process involving the county health teams, the disease programs, and the MOH's Supply Chain Management Unit (SCMU). The MOH piloted this approach throughout Liberia in collaboration with the Global Fund and other partners. PMI is supporting the planning and implementation of the interim approach in five counties through training, technical assistance, and logistical support, and at the central level through overall management support to the SCMU, and the secondment of an operations advisor to strengthen management of commodities at the NDS.

This collaborative effort has enhanced commodity security, accountability and availability for malaria, HIV/AIDS, reproductive health and essential drugs programs; however, much remains to be done. An evaluation of the interim approach planned for 2014 was postponed due to the Ebola crisis, and will be undertaken in 2015. Following the evaluation, PMI will support efforts to update and revise the Supply Chain Master plan developed in 2010 to ensure donor-supported capacity-building inputs are aligned with MOH priorities and strategies for assuring a more secure and transparent supply chain.

The LMIS data emanating from health facilities should feed into the database of the SCMU to inform forecasting, quantification, and procurement planning of health commodities. However, data quality remains unreliable and continues to make forecasting and quantification difficult, and these challenges have been inadvertently reinforced through the interim approach, which set up a parallel reporting system. The NMCP has recognized these problems and has increased its coordination with PMI to remedy the situation. Additionally, the Global Fund has committed resources to the rollout of the LMIS forms to eleven counties, complementing the effort of PMI in the four largest counties. Through the interim approach, the MOH is also piloting a new data form designed to collect more accurate consumption data on malaria commodities that is expected to inform a future revision of LMIS tools, as well as provide stronger evidence to inform future quantification of commodities. The present national quantification for antimalarials was largely derived from data retrieved from cross-referencing services data from the HMIS with demographic data. Local capacity to ensure country-led quantification exercises for antimalarials is crucial to PMI endeavors.

The managerial and supervisory capacity at the NMCP is being bolstered in order to ensure the long-term sustainability of malaria activities. The former deputy program manager was officially appointed as program manager at the NMCP in the fall of 2013. The deputy position will likely continue to be vacant until an organizational assessment is finalized as a Global Fund condition precedent. The NMCP has the opportunity moving forward to track program performance and implementation through its independent leadership.

In 2014 and early 2015, Liberia experienced an outbreak of Ebola Virus Disease (EVD). The outbreak began in March 2014 with cases crossing from Guinea to Liberia. The Ebola outbreak posed unprecedented challenges for Liberia's health system. Across the country, significant numbers of facilities closed during the height of the Ebola crisis, and the level of service provision and utilization of open health facilities dropped due to fear among both health workers and clients, with the most acute impact occurring between August and December 2014. This had a significant negative impact on access to malaria diagnosis and specific treatment– while the private sector played a role in continuing to provide access, the number of untreated cases may have increased. The EVD outbreak impacted the implementation of all malaria activities, but two of the biggest impacts were the postponement of the LLIN mass campaign from December 2014 to April 2015 and the adoption of WHO guidelines recommending clinical diagnosis and treatment of malaria.

With aid from the international community and concerted leadership from the GOL, the country began recording a decline in Ebola cases in early 2015, and the country was declared Ebola free May 9, 2015. On June 29, 2015, a confirmed case of Ebola was reported in a 17-year-old male who had died in Liberia. Five contacts associated with this case were confirmed to have Ebola, one of whom died. The last two patients were discharged on July 23 after testing negative for Ebola twice, and all contacts have now completed their 21-day monitoring period.

Though Ebola is still present in the region and holds the potential to be reintroduced, significant training and distribution of personal protective equipment has increased the probability that potential new cases would be recognized, isolated, and brought quickly under control. Supporting the restoration of health care and malaria services at all levels is a key priority for PMI, along with the broader USG support to Liberia, in the coming year. Continuing to ensure malaria services are available throughout Liberia will mean helping the health system respond to these changes and re-establishing, restoring, and strengthening clinical case management, diagnostics, supply chain, and community health service delivery. It may also mean looking more closely at the private sector, parts of which may have provided a crucial outlet for access to malaria treatment when health facilities were closed.

PMI investments in FY 2016 will be bolstered by additional support from the USG and other donors for restoration of health services and health system functioning following the Ebola outbreak. USAID, with resources under the FY 2015 Ebola supplemental funding, is expanding support for service delivery in at least 60 additional facilities and associated communities across three counties, and will provide additional support to the county health teams in six counties to strengthen management of the health system and expand community-based services, including iCCM. Coordination will be led by the NMCP and facilitated by the USAID Mission; a key feature is the use of the same implementing partners as PMI, thus ensuring that resources will be coordinated to increase overall coverage of key malaria interventions rather than duplicate them.

The Centers for Disease Control and Prevention (CDC) also has established a national program to support key activities under the Global Health Security Agenda, which will include a focus on strengthening surveillance, public health laboratory functions, and adherence to infection prevention and control standards. Global Health Security Agenda funding through CDC will help to build epidemiology skills within the public health system at both the national and county level. There will not be an explicit focus on malaria; however, broader improvements in the overall public health epidemiology and laboratory systems are expected to create opportunities for strengthening management of malaria services. PMI will work with both the USG and GOL and partner counterparts to ensure that the NMCP continues to be strengthened and supported – for instance, by inclusion of malaria service indicators in activities targeting restoration of the health system, and by supporting the inclusion of NMCP staff in the basic Field Epidemiology and LaboratoryTraining Program being established with support from CDC.

III. OPERATIONAL PLAN

The overall PMI support strategy for Liberia is nested within the GHI strategy for Liberia, which seeks to align, complement, and support Liberia's 2011-2021 National Health and Social Welfare Policy and Plan. To improve the overall health status of the population, strategic investments need to be made that take the best advantage of resources from government, development partners, and technical agencies.

PMI's national-level support includes health system strengthening, bolstering the HMIS and LMIS, improving pharmaceutical and commodity supply chain management, and enhancing BCC activities. Improving diagnostic capacity, promoting quality medicines, and supporting ITN distribution through ANC clinics and at institutional delivery, and antimalarial commodity distribution through health facilities, are among specific interventions that PMI will continue to support under its nationwide investment approach. In many cases, PMI is one partner among several others, enabling PMI to expand its activities beyond what could have been possible otherwise.

Support at the county level consists of the implementation of Liberia's Essential Package of Health Services at the facility and community levels through a government-to-government Fixed Amount Reimbursement Agreement (FARA). This is the principal delivery mechanism for preventive and curative malaria activities. Three counties are targeted for service delivery and an additional three counties may be targeted for strategic support to augment service delivery and decentralized system strengthening. These counties were prioritized in USAID/Liberia's five-year strategy based on their population concentration (the six counties account for 75% of the total population of Liberia) and their potential to fuel nationwide development. Several USAID funding streams, including HIV/AIDS, maternal and child health, and family planning, will be combined with PMI resources. Scale-up to nationwide coverage for activities will be achieved through coordination with the Global Fund, the multi-donor Pool Fund, and the European Union.

Accountability of PMI resources at the county level will be enhanced through MOH performance-based contracting of NGOs supported by PMI through the FARA. There are seven malaria specific indicators used to assess the performance of contracted NGOs under the FARA: management of malaria according to the standard malaria protocol, management of uncomplicated malaria, management of complicated malaria, availability of mosquito nets for ANC, availability of RDTs, availability of ACTs, and availability of SP. USAID visits each FARA county every quarter and randomly selects facilities for field monitoring. USAID uses baseline assessment documents and integrated supervision monitoring reports provided by the CHTs and partners to verify performance of the various health facilities under the FARA. In addition, HMIS indicators may be used evaluate the FARA, as both IPTp and treatment indicators are included as indicators in the performance-based financing scheme. Leading up to the Ebola crisis, HMIS data had shown continued improvements in service delivery within counties supported through the FARA, as well as those supported by other donors. For instance, IPTp2 coverage among pregnant women residing in catchment areas around USAID-supported facilities in Bong in 2012 was 79%, up from 70% the previous year. In Lofa, IPTp went from 45% to 58%.

As the current FARA will end in June 2015, plans are in place to implement a follow-on agreement with the MOH. The future agreement will maintain the key interventions, especially those related to malaria, and its design and indicators will be influenced by ongoing evaluations of the current FARA. Indicators for the new FARA will be discussed both in-country and with the headquarters M&E team in order to ensure full coverage of supported activities, in conjunction with PMI implementing partners, at both the health facility and community level.

Starting with FY 2016 funding, in addition to providing wrap around technical assistance for malaria service delivery, BCC, and M&E in USAID focus counties (Bong, Nimba and Lofa), PMI will provide targeted technical assistance for strengthening management and oversight of malaria service delivery, BCC and M&E in the Liberia's remaining 12 counties, where other donors support implementation of the activities themselves.

1. Insecticide-treated nets

NMCP/PMI objectives
In its Strategic Plan and Operational Guidelines on Long-Lasting Insecticidal Nets for Liberia 2012-2017, Liberia adopted a "universal coverage" goal for ITNs, defined operationally as one LLIN for each sleeping space or a maximum of three LLINs per household. The country has set objectives of 90% of families receiving at least one LLIN, and at least 85% of the general population sleeping under LLINs. Currently, mass campaigns are the main distribution method, reinforced by intense BCC at the community level. The NMCP also aims to complement campaigns with continuous distribution of nets during the first ANC visit and at the time of delivery in a registered health care institution to encourage delivery in facilities.

Progress since PMI was launched
Liberia was one of the first countries to distribute LLINs door-to-door through campaigns in combination with net "hang-up" in households. Between 2008 and 2014 nearly 4.6 million LLINs were distributed in Liberia through rolling campaigns, ANC services, and at institutional delivery, including approximately 1.7 million LLINs purchased by PMI.

Two mass LLIN campaigns occurred in Liberia in 2012 supported by PMI and the Global Fund. In total, approximately 1.3 million nets were distributed in nine counties as outlined in the table below. No campaigns took place in 2013 or 2014, but 80,000 LLINs were procured by the Global Fund and distributed to facilities in December of 2014 for distribution to women at their first ANC visit and at the time of delivery at the facility.

Table 3: LLIN Distribution by County through Campaigns in 2012

Bomi	Bong	Gbarpolu	Grand Bassa	Grand Cape Mount	Lofa	Margibi	Montserrado	Nimba	Total distributed	Total distributed by PMI
88,194 (Global Fund)	210,035 (Global Fund)	50,977 (PMI)	177,014 (Global Fund)	92,000 (PMI)	185,443 (Global Fund)	149,126 (PMI) 37,178 (Global Fund)	3,850 (PMI), 143,743 (Global Fund)	157,811 (Global Fund)	1,295,371	295,953

Results from the 2013 Liberia DHS indicated that the number of households owning at least one ITN increased from 50% in 2011 to 55% in 2013. Additionally, although there was a small decrease in the number of urban households owning at least one ITN, from 52% in 2011 to 50% in 2013, the percentage of rural households that owned at least one ITN increased markedly over the same period from 47% to 61%. ITN use rates among populations with access to an ITN were observed to be 86% in 2013[7], indicating that even after the 2012 campaigns Liberia continued to have an ITN access constraint, rather than an ITN-use behavior problem.

A PMI-supported qualitative assessment of ownership of mass distribution campaign nets was conducted in 2014 to explore possible reasons for low LLIN ownership despite repeated mass campaigns. Data were collected from four communities in Grand Cape Mount and Gbarpolu where PMI-supported LLIN distribution campaigns took place in 2012. A main finding was that not every household received the number of nets they were eligible to receive. A variety of monitoring- and distribution-related problems were identified that contributed to this outcome (e.g., poor working relationships between the NGO distributors and county and district health teams, inaccurate enumeration of sleeping spaces, incomplete coverage of some communities and/or households, and insufficient availability of nets). The assessment also confirmed that LLIN usage was related to access, with the proportion of sleeping spaces that were covered in the four communities averaging 53% (ranging from 29% to 69%).

Recognizing that the LLIN distribution system in Liberia had faced significant challenges including weak tracking of net distribution by counties and sporadic coverage of districts and counties, in 2013 the NMCP opted to revise its strategy and plan its first-ever national mass LLIN distribution campaign, replacing the strategy of phased campaigns.

Progress during the last 12-18 months

Liberia was originally scheduled to conduct its first nationwide mass campaign during the last quarter of 2014. However, the EVD outbreak forced Liberia to rethink its strategy for the mass campaign, given that people would not be able to gather at central distribution points and that surveyors would not be able to enter households to do proper enumeration. Under the constraints of the EVD outbreak, the campaign was delayed until April 2015 with a door-to-door strategy of supplying three LLINs per household. PMI supported campaign planning, including helping to finalize the campaign action plan, timeline, budget, and supporting tools and documents. Approximately 2.8 million nets procured by the Global Fund were distributed throughout Liberia between April and June 2015.

In addition, in 2014 PMI procured 250,000 LLINs for continuous distribution through ANC clinics and at institutional delivery, and over the last year national level supportive supervision monitoring teams were formed and oriented to support ANC/institutional delivery distribution at health facilities. Furthermore, PMI supported the development of continuous distribution documentation, including a supportive supervision checklist and a monthly county-level, supportive supervision reporting template.

---

[7] LLIN Use and Access for PMI Countries. VectorWorks/JHUCCP. April 2015.

Implementation of continuous distribution has been ongoing for less than a year. The first 80,000 LLINs to be distributed through continuous distribution at ANC clinics and at institutional delivery were delivered in December 2014. As of April 2015, six counties had received ANC/institutional delivery LLINs and started implementation. The remaining nine counties are to receive LLINs and start supportive supervision implementation in July 2015.

Commodity gap analysis

Table 4: ITN Gap Analysis

Calendar Year	2015	2016	2017
Total targeted population	4,035,433	4,120,177	4,206,701
Continuous Distribution Needs			
Channel #1: ANC[1]	181,594	185,408	189,302
Channel #2: Institutional delivery[2]	131,152	133,906	136,718
Estimated Total Need for Continuous	312,746	319,314	326,020
Mass Distribution Needs			
2015 mass distribution campaign	2,800,000	0	0
Estimated Total Need for Campaigns	2,800,000	0	0
Total Calculated Need: Routine and Campaign	**3,112,746**	**319,314**	**326,020**
Partner Contributions			
ITNs carried over from previous year	0	0	10,686
ITNs from Global Fund Consolidated Grant	2,800,000	0	0
ITNs planned with PMI funding	413,850	330,000	320,000
Total ITNs Available	3,213,850	330,000	330,686
Total ITN Surplus (Gap)	101,104[3]	10,686	4,666

[1]5% of national population pregnant in a given year with 90% ANC coverage; [2]65% pregnant women deliver in an institution

[3]The net surplus in 2015 is being used to fill a gap in the 2015 mass LLIN campaign that arose during distribution when three nets were distributed per room, instead of per household, in some areas.

Plans and justification

PMI will support post-distribution activities for the recently completed 2015 nationwide mass campaign, including a post-distribution campaign survey (at six months) and BCC for consistent and correct LLIN use and care. In addition, PMI will support planning for Liberia's next universal coverage mass campaign, which should take place in 2018. Furthermore, PMI will continue to support routine distribution of LLINs by procuring LLINs to cover ANC and institutional delivery needs, and transporting the nets down to the county level as a national system is not yet in place to move routine LLINs to county warehouses. In addition, PMI will provide technical support for the institutionalization and evaluation of these routine distribution methods. Specifically, in 2015/2016 PMI will support a review of the first year of implementation of Liberia's continuous distribution system and provide suggestions for improvements.

Proposed activities with FY 2016 funding: **($1,872,000)**

- Procure LLINs. PMI will procure approximately 320,000 LLINs for distribution through ANC visits and at delivery in a health care institution, which will meet Liberia's routine distribution needs for calendar year 2017. ($1,152,000)

- Distribute LLINs. PMI will support routine LLIN distribution in all 15 counties, including warehousing and transportation down to the county level, and will provide technical assistance to the MOH to plan distribution down to the facility level through existing county distribution mechanisms. The plan is for two distributions per year to facilities that provide ANC services and/or institutional delivery. The NMCP will supply nets to the counties, and then county health teams will supply facilities based on identified gaps from monitoring visits. ($320,000)

- Technical assistance for continuous distribution and for 2018 mass campaign planning. PMI will fund technical assistance to help the NMCP continue to institutionalize LLIN distribution through ANC clinics and at institutions through supportive supervision and an M&E plan to track distribution of nets and reordering needs. PMI will support training of national level supervisors and printing of checklists and registers. In addition, PMI will support planning for Liberia's next universal, nationwide mass campaign in 2018. ($400,000)

2. Indoor residual spraying and entomological monitoring

NMCP/PMI objectives

The 2010-2015 revised NMCP strategy included increased use of IRS in rural districts with high malaria prevalence, covering approximately 50% of the population, in order to quickly reduce malaria transmission. IRS was to be used to complement LLINs to reduce malaria prevalence, morbidity, and mortality; however, no IRS has been implemented in Liberia since 2013.

Progress since PMI was launched

PMI supported IRS in Liberia from 2009 to 2013. As part of the IRS program, PMI collaborated with private companies to support implementation of IRS. The Arcelor Mittal Steel Company conducted three rounds of spraying in its concession areas in Nimba and Grand Bassa counties from 2010 to 2012, and the Liberia Agriculture Company supported one round of spraying in its concessional area in Grand Bassa County in 2011. PMI provided insecticides and technical support, including training and mentoring, to these companies to build capacity to conduct IRS.

The last time IRS was conducted, PMI supported spraying with a long-lasting organophosphate due to the observation of significant pyrethroid resistance throughout Liberia and the requirement to spray carbamates twice during the malaria transmission season because of their short residual life. However, because of the higher cost of the long-lasting organophosphate, only 10% of the Liberian population could be protected with IRS in 2013, compared with 23% of the population on a similar budget the previous year. Therefore, after consultations within the PMI interagency team and discussions with the NMCP, the decision was made to suspend PMI-supported IRS in Liberia, and instead focus on increased entomological monitoring and universal LLIN coverage since even in areas of pyrethroid resistance, LLINs act as a physical barrier and the irritancy of pyrethroids on the nets may still reduce mosquito blood-feeding. Although PMI support for IRS ended in 2013, the NMCP has expressed interest in working with private sector sources to support IRS for their populations.

In early 2014 a shipping container was modified for use as an insectary situated next to the NMCP. The insectary has an adult room, a larval room, and a workroom where resistance tests can be conducted. Having a functional insectary situated next to the NMCP office and developing a rotational schedule for routine surveillance, annual insecticide resistance monitoring, insectary maintenance and active collaboration with other partners, such as the MENTOR Initiative, U.S. Naval Medical Research Unit No. 3, and Armed Forces of Liberia, has provided an opportunity for the vector control unit staff to become more focused in their entomological monitoring work.

Below is a table summarizing PMI's support for IRS in Liberia from 2009 to 2013.

Table 5: PMI-supported IRS activities 2009 – 2013

Calendar Year	Number of Districts Sprayed	Insecticide Used	Number of Structures Sprayed	Coverage Rate	Population Protected
2009	2	pyrethroid	~22,000		~160,000
2010	4	pyrethroid	52,468	98%	420,532
2011	5	pyrethroid and carbamate	89,710	96%	834,671
2012	5	pyrethroid and carbamate	96,901	98%	869,707
2013	1	organophosphate	42,708	96%	367,930

Progress during the last 12-18 months

Over the past year PMI supported the NMCP to evaluate the spatial and temporal composition of anopheline mosquitoes at two sites in Liberia (i.e., Tomato Camp in Bong County and Franktown in Montserrado County) through pyrethrum spray collections, human landing catches, and CDC light traps. In addition, insecticide susceptibility testing was supported at six sites. PMI also supported an entomologist to sit with the NMCP to help build capacity for entomological surveillance, and when the PMI-supported entomologist left Liberia due to the EVD outbreak, the NMCP technicians stepped up and continued mosquito collections on their own, including conducting resistance testing on their own for the first time in Maryland county and completing testing of all four insecticide classes in Grand Cape Mount, Grand Bassa, and Montserrado counties.

Where insecticide susceptibility testing has been conducted, significant pyrethroid and DDT resistance has been found in Liberia.

Table 6: 2014 WHO Bioassay Results for *An. gambiae* s.l. – 24-hour Mortality Rates

County	Site	Bendiocarb	DDT	Deltamethrin	Fenitrothion
Monrovia	Parkers corner	99 (100)	27 (100)	46 (100)	95 (100)
Bong	SKT	95 (100)	27 (100)	15 (128)	100 (102)
Grand Gedeh	Zwedru	98 (100)	30 (100)	62 (100)	100 (100)
Grand Bassa	Bokay Town	99 (100)	54 (100)	78 (100)	100 (100)
Cape Mount	Nimba Point	na	16 (100)	36 (100)	na
Maryland	Harper (Old and New Kru Town)	98 (100)	29 (100)	65 (100)	100 (100)

Greater than 98% mortality in tube bioassays indicates full susceptibility, 90-97% mortality indicates probable resistance, and less than 90% mortality indicates resistance to the insecticide being tested. Numbers tested are in parentheses.

Plans and justification

PMI will continue to assist the NMCP in setting up a comprehensive mosquito surveillance program. Other partners collecting entomological data in Liberia include the Liberian Institute for Biomedical Research and the MENTOR Initiative, which is currently evaluating the impact of non-pyrethroid insecticide-treated durable wall linings on vector density and malaria incidence. All relevant data will be shared among partners. Specifically, PMI will work to characterize insecticide susceptibility in Liberia's five regions. As of 2014 resistance data had been collected from five of Liberia's fifteen counties plus Monrovia. In 2015, resistance data will be collected from six additional counties, and in 2016 the remaining four counties will be surveyed. In 2017, PMI will support insecticide resistance surveillance in 11 counties. PMI will also continue to support the determination of the spatial and temporal composition and distribution of anopheline species, as well as maintain and support a functional insectary.

Proposed activities with FY 2016 funding: **($529,000)**

- Increase NMCP entomology capacity by providing equipment, supplies, and mentoring for NMCP entomology technicians. PMI will provide mosquito surveillance equipment to the NMCP to enable them to scale-up mosquito density, behavior, species identification, and insecticide resistance activities. Entomological monitoring will be conducted monthly at three sites and resistance testing will occur annually at 11 sites, covering the five geographic regions of the country. PMI will also support a full-time entomologist to sit with the NMCP to help build capacity and support on-the-job training. In addition, PMI will continue to support the maintenance of the container insectary established in 2014. ($500,000)

- Technical assistance for vector control activities. CDC staff will conduct two technical assistance (TA) visits to assist with training and to monitor planning and implementation of vector control activities. Mosquito surveillance activities, including use of WHO tube and CDC bottle assays and mosquito collection techniques, and morphological identifications, will be reviewed. ($29,000)

3. Malaria in pregnancy

NMCP/PMI objectives

The NMCP is currently in the process of validating/costing its National Strategic Plan for 2016 through 2020. The country's policy on MIP is a three-pronged approach, which consists of prompt and effective case management of malaria and anemia, IPTp with more than two doses of SP, and use of LLINs. Current objectives related to MIP include:
- At least 80% of pregnant women attending antenatal consultation receive at least two doses of SP for IPTp according to the national MIP protocol;
- 100% of health facilities have SP available with no stockout lasting more than one week.
- At least 80% of pregnant women attending antenatal consultation receive a LLIN;
- At least 85% of women of child-bearing age sleep under LLINs; and

- At least 80% of pregnant women have access to prompt and effective treatment of MIP according to the national MIP protocol.

The MIP program at the NMCP is still very donor dependent. PMI and the Global fund remain the biggest donors supporting the NMCP to meet its objectives.

With the support of PMI, and based on WHO's guidance, the NMCP has changed the policy for treatment of malaria in pregnancy from oral quinine as the first-line treatment for uncomplicated malaria throughout all trimesters to oral quinine in the first trimester and use of ACTs in the second and third trimester. However the actual implementation of this policy at the health facility level has not been rolled out. Treatment protocols have been updated but health workers are not yet trained, hence at health facilities, health workers continue to administer quinine to pregnant women during all trimesters for treatment of uncomplicated malaria. The plan to train, disseminate, and reproduce treatment guidelines did not happen in 2014 due to the outbreak of EVD. In 2015, with PMI's support, health workers will be trained on the new policy. In addition,PMI will support the printing and dissemination of new treatment protocols and guidelines in all 15 counties.

In addition, iron/folic acid is distributed to pregnant women during ANC visits. The current formulation contains 200 mg dried ferrous sulfate to 65 mg ferrous iron and 0.25 mg folic acid or 0.4 mg folic acid. This presentation complies with the WHO recommendation for daily administration.

Progress since PMI was launched
Since the introduction of IPTp in Liberia in 2005, there has been increasing coverage parallel to gradual increases in access to health care. While uptake of IPTp2 has increased nationally from 4.5% in 2005 to 48% in 2013, availability of SP at health facilities remains a challenge – an issue believed to be associated with supply chain problems, as well as overuse of SP as prophylaxis by non-targeted populations. The overuse of SP as prophylaxis and treatment for non-targeted populations was reported during supervisory visits in private health facilities in early 2014 in Margibi and Montserrado counties. SP was being prescribed not only to pregnant women during ANC, but also to patients presenting with fever in the absence of ACTs. This is not NMCP policy, and the issue is currently being addressed by the NMCP, which has formed a response team for mentoring and coaching visits to health facilities that receive negative feedback during supervisory visits on adherence and use of monotherapy for malaria treatment.

Community outreach efforts by certified midwives have delivered ANC services, including SP as recommended by Liberia's MIP guidelines, to pregnant women residing more than five kilometers from health facilities.

PMI has supported the training of 390 gCHVs of the 1,587 who are within USAID focus counties. PMI supported the development of training manuals and protocols used in the training of these gCHVs, as well as the training of trained traditional midwives. PMI supported the revision of core competencies in the new national curricula of pre-service training institutions by updating the malaria section of the Tropical and Communicable Disease Course. The malaria component of The Handbook for Health Workers in Liberia was also revised. In addition, PMI has supported IEC/BBC at the community level through reproduction of comprehensive community health education materials that promote ANC attendance and the importance of prevention of malaria during pregnancy, as well as nationwide radio campaigns and printing of posters on MIP.

Since FY 2012, PMI has supported performance-based financing initiatives through sub-contracts to non-governmental organizations in USAID focus counties. The performance-based financing scheme has contributed to improvements in ANC attendance, among other maternal health related indicators. In 2013, the proportion of pregnant women having at least four ANC visits with a skilled provider was 75% in Nimba, 70% in Lofa, and 59% in Bong. IPTp2 rates were 54% in Bong, 52% in Nimba, and 48% in Lofa. Stockouts of SP, in part due to the moratorium on commodities in 2013 and weak follow-up of pregnant women, may explain the discrepancy between IPTp2 rates and the high proportion of women having at least four ANC visits.

Progress during the last 12-18 months
During the past two years, PMI assisted the NMCP in finalizing updated MIP protocols and treatment guidelines based on new recommendation released by WHO in 2012. These new guidelines were harmonized across all MIP and case management related documents, including the national pre-service curriculum, in-service community training materials, BCC module materials, and supervision and M&E tools. These documents were revised for nationwide use.

Insufficient progress has been made with IPTp coverage from 2014 to 2015 mainly due to the impact of EVD. Access to ANC services, as well as safe institutional deliveries, was reduced during the past year as a result of closure of health facilities. Also as a result of EVD, the yearly training plan for gCHVs was put on hold in late 2014 and will be resumed in 2015.

Commodity gap analysis

Table 6. SP Gap Analysis for Malaria in Pregnancy

Calendar Year	2015	2016	2017
Total population	4,035,433	4,120,177	4,206,701
SP Needs			
Total number of pregnant women attending ANC[1]	181,594	185,408	189,302
Total SP Need (in treatments)[2]	**381,348**	**389,357**	**397,533**
Partner Contributions			
SP carried over from previous year	0	534,878	534,878
SP from Global Fund	759,559	0	0
SP planned with PMI funding	156,667	389,357	0
Total SP Available	**916,226**	**924,235**	**534,878**
Total SP Surplus (Gap)	**534,878**	**534,878**	**137,345**

[1] 5% of national population pregnant in a given year with 90% ANC coverage (NMCP target of 90% ANC coverage over the next three years)
[2] Percentage of pregnant women receiving one to four doses of IPTp is 80%, 70%, 40%, 20%, respectively (NMCP communication 2015)

Plans and justification

PMI proposes to build on the gains made from 2012 to 2013. Results from the 2013 DHS indicate that 96% of women who gave birth in the five years preceding the survey received care from a skilled provider at least once for their last birth. According to the 2013 DHS, 78% of women had at least four ANC visits. The MOH, through the NMCP, the Family Health Division, the Community Health Division, and the Health Promotion Unit, continue to make efforts to improve the quality of ANC service delivery throughout the country at health facilities and ANC attendance through outreach efforts. PMI will continue to provide technical assistance to support the NMCP in the implementation, scale-up, and monitoring of MIP, including implementation of the new IPTp guidelines:

- The implementation of the revised MIP guidelines will be scaled-up and monitored using revised M&E tools.
- An assessment will be conducted to evaluate the introduction of the new MIP guidelines in health facilities (public and private) offering ANC services.
- LLINs will be procured and distributed nationwide to all pregnant women during ANC visits and at delivery.

- SP will continue to be the drug of choice for IPTp and will be administered according to the new guidelines released by WHO; PMI will work with the NMCP and Global Fund to ensure that the SP need for 2016 and 2017 is met in the NMCP's revised procurement and supply management plan to be submitted during the third quarter of 2015.
- Pregnant women with malaria symptoms will be tested and treated as directed by the national standard treatment guidelines.
- The supply chain and management system will be strengthened to ensure availability of LLINs, SP, and antimalarial drugs in all targeted health facilities.
- BCC for MIP will be strengthened, including BCC aimed at health care workers on the importance of having medication on site and avoiding stockouts, BCC at the community level regarding use of SP for the prevention of malaria in pregnant women, and BCC to discourage off-label use of SP by health care workers and the public.

Proposed activities with FY 2016 funding: **($750,000)**

- <u>In-service training and supervision for health care workers at ANC facilities.</u> In-service training and supervision of health care workers at ANC facilities and in the community through the performance-based financing initiative will continue. As in previous years, funding will be channeled to the MOH through a FARA with the GOL for performance-based contracts with NGOs. This will include in-service training and supervision of health providers in targeted health facilities. In addition, support will be provided for the MOH and CHTs to supervise health facilities in focus counties every quarter. Funding from the Global Fund, the GOL, and other donors support implementation of similar activities in the remaining, non-PMI supported counties. ($450,000)

- <u>Improve quality of care and adherence to standards for MIP in USAID focus counties.</u> This activity is focused on strengthening quality assurance/quality improvement through technical assistance for supportive supervision in the three USAID focus counties, Nimba, Lofa, and Bong, at the facility level for improving MIP practices. This activity also includes support to the Liberian Board of Nursing and Midwifery to integrate MIP activities into practical training activities at the central level and joint monitoring and supervision visits of six training sites for certified midwives. ($100,000)

- <u>Improve quality of care and adherence to standards for MIP in non-focus counties.</u> This activity is focused on strengthening quality assurance/quality improvement through technical assistance for supportive supervision in Liberia's other 12 counties at the facility level for improving MIP practices. ($200,000)

4. Case management

a. Diagnosis and Treatment

NMCP/PMI objectives
The Liberia National Strategic Plan 2010-2015 adheres to the WHO recommendation for parasitological confirmation of all suspected uncomplicated malaria cases and prompt effective treatment of positive cases with an ACT. To achieve the malaria diagnostic testing and treatment

objectives of the Strategic Plan, the NMCP plans to support the scale-up of malaria diagnostics in all public and private health facilities regardless of operational level, in private medicine stores and pharmacies, and in the community by gCHVs and community health workers (CHWs) delivering integrated community case management (iCCM). In addition, in collaboration with the National Public Health Reference Laboratory/National Diagnostics Unit (NPHRL/NDU) and the County Diagnostics Supervisors, the NMCP plans to continue improving the quality of malaria diagnostic testing through on-site training and supportive supervision in all fifteen counties. PMI will support the NMCP to focus on RDT use at the primary level (health posts and community) and quality microscopy at hospitals and health centers.

According to the MOH's 2012 Technical Guidelines on Malaria Case Management, the first-line treatment for uncomplicated malaria in infants > 5 kg, adolescents, and adults is fixed-dose artesunate-amodiaquine. Oral quinine is the first-line treatment for infants < 5 kg and in pregnant women in their first trimester. With the support of PMI, the NMCP has changed the policy for treatment of malaria in pregnancy based on WHO's guidance from oral quinine as the first-line treatment for uncomplicated malaria throughout all trimesters to oral quinine in the first trimester and use of ACTs in the second and third trimester. In 2015, health workers will be trained on the new policy and implementation will be rolled out.

For severe malaria, the 2012 guidelines added intramuscular (IM)/intravenous (IV) artesunate to intravenous quinine and intramuscular artemether as first-line treatments. Among these three medications, no preferred treatment is specified. Both IM quinine and IM artemether are listed as options for pre-referral treatment in rural areas where IV infusion is not possible. Rectal artesunate is not in the national guidelines and not used in Liberia; however, in the future, the NMCP intends on adding this to the guidelines for pre-referral treatment.

Progress since PMI was launched
As of 2013, the MOH provided malaria diagnostics and treatment drugs to all public facilities and all private facilities that provide diagnostic and treatment services through a memorandum of understanding that requires facilities to report via the HMIS. With support from Comic Relief, and later the USAID Office of Foreign Disaster Assistance, the MENTOR Initiative has worked with the NMCP since 2013 to train and supply subsidized RDTs and ACTs through registered private retail pharmacies and drug stores in Montserrado County (where a majority of these outlets operate). Continuation and expansion of this activity is supported in the Global Fund Round 10 Award. The NMCP is also working with the Community Health Division at the MOH to reach children less than five years of age in hard to reach areas (>5 km from a fixed health facility) with RDTs and ACTs through gCHVs and iCCM. At the community level, the ratio of gCHVs to community dwellers has increased to one gCHV for every 500 people, up from one gCHV per 1,000 people. This has contributed to progress in diagnosing and treating uncomplicated malaria at the community level in hard-to-reach locations and to increased referrals of persistent febrile cases to health facilities.

PMI funded nationwide implementation of an outreach training and supportive supervision program for facility-based malaria diagnosis from 2010-2012. During this program, trained laboratory supervisors visited facilities on a quarterly basis to provide onsite mentoring and training. PMI purchased and funded the distribution of microscopes (including two multi-head training microscopes), parts, bulbs, fuses, glass slides, and Giemsa stain to facilities that had microscopy capacity.

Liberia has made improvements in data collection and reporting through the HMIS in terms of the numbers of suspected malaria cases tested and positive cases treated. According to HMIS data, the proportion of reported malaria cases confirmed with a laboratory test has steadily increased from 62% and 79% in 2011 and 2012 respectively, to 82% in 2013. In addition, in 2013 the HMIS system reported administration of 1.2 million artemisinin-based combination therapy (ACT) treatments, which represents 81% of the estimated 1.48 million malaria cases reported that were either clinically diagnosed or positive by microscopy or RDT. These figures are almost certain to represent only a portion of the projected need because they overlap with a temporary moratorium on procurement of case management commodities.

In 2013, 730 health workers were trained in malaria diagnosis and treatment, resulting in 3,579 health workers trained since 2011. Personnel at 647 facilities require training to achieve national scale.

The Liberia Medicines and Health Products Regulatory Authority (LMHRA), established with support from PMI in 2010, has been addressing the problem of drug quality. Significant quantities of poor quality medicines have been removed from commercial medicine stores and pharmacies and destroyed by the LMHRA following quality control testing. In addition, medicines imported into Liberia that do not meet the full registration requirements established by the LMHRA for the importation of medicines are confiscated and destroyed. The Inspectorate of the LHMRA has also been supportive in removing diverted drugs and health commodities found in commercial medicine stores and pharmacies that are donated by donors and partners. These commodities are returned to the NDS for redistribution to public health facilities across Liberia.

Progress during the last 12-18 months

Most of the planned activities for expansion of case management were adversely affected by the 2014 Ebola epidemic, which resulted in a significant disruption of the entire health system for months. Diagnostic testing and access to appropriate treatment fell off dramatically in the last half of 2014 as a result of the Ebola epidemic and adoption in September 2014 of WHO guidelines temporarily recommending clinical diagnosis and treatment of malaria at all levels of care and suspending diagnostic testing in settings that lacked appropriate infection prevention control training and personal protective equipment. This temporary suspension remains in effect, at least until July 2015, though significant progress has been made with expansion of infection prevention training and personal protective equipment distribution.

In order to increase the coverage of malaria diagnostics and treatment, in 2013 the NMCP conducted a mapping of gCHVs in all 15 counties in Liberia. Based on the mapping exercise, it was determined that there were approximately 8,000 gCHVs nationwide who were tasked with providing malaria diagnostics and treatment coverage for hard-to-reach communities that are greater than 5 km from a health facility. Between 2012 and 2013, 3,727 of the gCHVs were trained in malaria case management as part of iCCM. The role of gCHVs in malaria case management is to offer ACTs upon RDT confirmation of malaria and, in the case of severe disease, referral to a higher level of care. The gCHVs also perform house-to-house education on a range of malaria topics, including the proper use of ITNs and management of fever in children less than five years of age. Nationwide, in addition to gCHVs, there are 2,396 Community Health Committees and 2,022 Community Health Development Committees that were established to encourage community responsibility, ownership, and participation in health and social welfare. Although gCHVs should receive regular supervisory visits from the facility, this has not yet occurred. The Community Health Development Committees were expected to scale up this activity but plans were interrupted by the EVD outbreak.

Plans for supervising gCHVs, as well as plans for expanding iCCM to Grand Kru County were not implemented in 2014 because of the disruption caused by the Ebola epidemic. In addition, the gCHVs who remained active or returned to work have suspended diagnostic testing. Following the 2014 Ebola epidemic, the MOH and partners reconsidered the role of volunteers across the health sector and elaborated a plan to transition iCCM activities to remunerated CHWs over the period 2015-2017. One of the USAID/Liberia Mission's bilateral programs will support the MOH to pilot a compensation scheme for CHWs.

Liberia has also adopted a policy to promote diagnostic testing with RDTs and first-line treatment in private medical stores and pharmacies. This will be accomplished by expanding a pilot program, which was conducted in approximately 200 outlets (Bushrod Island and Paynesville communities), to all of Montserrado County where nearly all the approximately 700 registered pharmacies and drug stores in Liberia operate. The pilot showed that with appropriate training, supervision, and adequate supplies, private vendors adhered to case management guidelines. However, the planned expansion was interrupted by the Ebola epidemic. USAID's Office of Foreign Disaster Assistance provided emergency funding to continue the provision of ACTs through private retail outlets, including supporting infection prevention control and triage in the context of EVD. Global Fund Round 10 resources will be used to continue/expand this activity following selection of an appropriate subrecipient.

Central level capacity strengthening for malaria diagnosis at the NPHRL/NDU continued in 2013 and early 2014. With PMI support, indicators for monitoring and supervision of malaria diagnostics quality have been included in an integrated laboratory supervision tool. The integrated supervision tool will be used by county diagnostic supervisors to monitor the availability and quality of facility-based malaria diagnostics. Furthermore, in March 2014, PMI sponsored three previously-certified WHO Level 1 microscopists to attend the WHO microscopy competency assessment course in Nairobi, Kenya, for recertification. A renewal of WHO microscopy certification is required every three years, and these individuals were last certified in 2010. Results from the re-certification course indicate that the three individuals are now certified at Levels 3 and 4. Therefore, an external trainer provided refresher training in June 2014 for the 15 county diagnostic supervisors and to further support the training of the 3 previously WHO certified microscopists. The plan to support cascade training of hospital and health facility laboratory microscopists was interrupted by the EVD outbreak. As laboratory services in general have been interrupted over the last year due to EVD, there are currently plans to conduct a refresher for the county diagnostic officers in 2015 and resume support for the MOH's de-centralization plan by supporting the cascade refresher trainings by the county diagnostic officers for hospital and health center laboratorians and on site supportive supervision.

Inconsistent supplies of diagnostic and treatment commodities at the facility level, despite availability in county and central stores, remain a major obstacle to access to diagnostic testing. Between May and August 2013, a temporary moratorium was placed by PMI and the Global Fund on supply and distribution of malaria commodities, including RDTs and ACTs, pending a review of the supply chain to address problems of leakages and stockouts. As a result of the review, an interim approach was adopted to strengthen commodity distribution and improve internal controls. The ongoing suspension of diagnostic testing for malaria in response to the 2014 Ebola epidemic will require reorienting health workers and supervisors, facility-by-facility, as they achieve adequate infection prevention control, and training and working with the NGOs that are supporting the hospitals and health centers to establish a resilient health system. Additional emphasis on the aspects of infection prevention and control and waste management will need to be developed and incorporated into training for health workers and supervisors.

In addition to supply chain constraints, inadequate collection and analyses of consumption data and trends resulted in diagnostic supplies not being adjusted as needed, resulting in stockouts. However, with increased reporting and use of HMIS data, improved data collection under the interim approach, and logistics management information system (LMIS) strengthening efforts, an opportunity exists to address these challenges, particularly as post-Ebola reconstruction resources become available as well. Additionally, a Supply Chain Management Unit (SCMU) has been established within the MOH that will work to streamline procurement, stock management, and distribution in a manner that will prevent or minimize stockouts and leakages. Unfortunately, the disruption in health service delivery that occurred in 2014 means that these reforms have yet to provide lasting impact and improved information for planning.

High staff turnover in health facilities and a high attrition rate among gCHVs continue to present challenges to rolling out malaria diagnostics. This has been severely exacerbated by the loss of large numbers of health workers during and following the Ebola epidemic. While some staff remain in the health system, and therefore are not lost, these high turnover rates mean more resources are continuously needed to improve malaria diagnostics capacity. Investments in community health services, including iCCM, planned through PMI, Ebola supplemental funding, and other donors and partners seek to support MOH priorities around building up Liberia's community health workforce, including creating a career path for gCHVs to become remunerated CHWs, which should help with retention, while also ensuring adequate numbers of both cadres of workers (gCHVs and CHWs).

PMI has provided training for personnel in the quality control laboratory of LMHRA and has procured equipment and supplies to ensure the continued functioning of the laboratory. The number of staff at LMHRA grew from 42 in 2013 to 48 in 2014, and all received training in post-marked surveillance. LMHRA has been instrumental in seizing antimalarial monotherapies and removing them from circulation and developing a database of adverse drug reactions. Liberia's quality control laboratory ranked number one among 12 participating African countries by the Network of Official Medicine Control Laboratories.

Commodity gap analysis

Table 7: RDT Gap Analysis

Calendar Year	2015	2016	2017
RDT Needs			
Target population at risk for malaria[1]	4,035,433	4,120,177	4,206,701
Total number projected fever cases[2]	7,457,480	7,614,087	7,773,983
Total number of projected fever cases seeking care in public sector[3]	4,474,488	4,568,452	4,664,390
Percent of fever cases confirmed with microscopy[4]	20%	20%	20%
Percent of fever cases confirmed with RDT[4]	80%	80%	80%
Total number of projected fever cases tested via iCCM[5]	298,299	304,563	310,959
Total RDT Needs	**3,877,890**	**3,959,325**	**4,042,471**
Partner Contributions			
RDTs carried over from previous year	0	0	0
RDTs from Global Fund	332,310	0	0
RDTs planned with PMI funding	1,750,000	2,957,000	1,400,000
Total RDTs Available	**2,082,310**	**2,957,000**	**1,400,000**
Total RDT Surplus (Gap)[6]	**(1,795,580)**	**(1,002,325)**	**(2,642,471)**

[1]Total population at risk for malaria, 2008 population census, 2.1% population growth rate
[2]Assumption 3.5 fevers in under-fives (16.1%), 2.5 fevers in 5-14 year olds (29.7%), 1 fever in 15+ (54.2%); population breakdown based on 2013 DHS
[3]80% seek care and of these 75% seek care in the public sector; public sector includes private sector facilities receiving drugs from NDS (Quantification Report May 2014)

[4]Global Fund PSM Plan 2013

[5]80% seek care and of these 5% seek care in the community (NMCP 2013 Consolidated Gap Analysis)
[6]The need calculated here for 2015 does not take into account the suspension of diagnostic services that took place in Liberia because of the EVD outbreak

Table 8: ACT Gap Analysis

Calendar Year	2015	2016	2017
ACT Needs			
Target population at risk for malaria[1]	4,035,433	4,120,177	4,206,701
Total number projected fever cases[2]	7,457,480	7,614,087	7,773,983
Total number of projected fever cases seeking care in public sector[3]	4,474,488	4,568,452	4,664,390
Total number of projected fever cases tested via iCCM[4]	298,299	304,563	310,959
Total projected number of malaria cases[5]	2,672,761	2,728,889	2,786,196
Total ACT Needs[6]	**2,903,764**	**2,964,743**	**3,027,002**
Partner Contributions			
ACTs carried over from previous year	0	0	2,379,418
ACTs from Global Fund	65,021	3,076,299	0
ACTs planned with PMI funding	2,650,825	2,267,862	1,000,000
Total ACTs Available	**2,715,846**	**5,344,161**	**3,379,418**
Total ACT Surplus (Gap)	**(187,918)**	**2,379,418**	**352,416**

[1]Total population at risk for malaria, 2008 population census, 2.1% population growth rate
[2]Assupmtion 3.5 fevers in under-fives (16.1%), 2.5 fevers in 5-14 year olds (29.7%), 1 fever in 15+ (54.2%); population breakdown based on 2013 DHS
[3]80% seek care and of these 75% seek care in the public sector; public sector includes private sector facilities receiving drugs from NDS (Quantification Report May 2014)

[4]80% seek care and of these 5% seek care in the community (NMCP 2013 Consolidated Gap Analysis)
[5]56% of tested fevers are positive for malaria (Quantification Report May 2014); note that cases are increasing due to population growth and that any effects of increasing ITN coverage were not factored into these calculations
[6]Total ACT needs is malaria cases plus 11% noncompliance (negative cases still treated with ACTs)

Plans and justification
PMI will provide support for laboratories, and in collaboration with the Global Fund, will work to strengthen the diagnostic capacity of the MOH. For malaria diagnostics, the program plans to initially train one county diagnostics supervisor for each of the 15 counties. These supervisors

will then conduct supervision activities in their respective counties primarily by on-site supervision. The number of health workers to be trained under this program depends on staff available to be trained and/or supervisor and staff turnover. PMI has an ongoing survey to assess staffing and equipment levels to inform the program on gaps to be addressed. As of 2015, there are an estimated 10,000 to 11,000 health care workers nationwide. This number includes public and private facility staff, covering both diagnostics and treatment.

PMI will continue to support the NMCP's efforts to expand access to malaria case management through iCCM and partnerships with private health care facilities. PMI, Global Fund, UNICEF and Ebola supplemental funding will all be used to support the scale-up of iCCM implementation. Coordination will be led by the NMCP and facilitated by the USAID/Liberia Mission. The approach includes training, supervision, and support for management at the central, county, and local levels, including harmonization of strategies and procedures across the MOH to ensure coherence among donor and partner investments. The Global Fund is providing full support for iCCM training across Liberia. PMI will also continue to provide technical assistance to NMCP efforts, in collaboration with the Global Fund and the MENTOR Initiative, to support scale-up of the private sector initiative to increase access to RDT testing before treatment and ACTs for those that test positive at medicine stores and pharmacies. PMI will also procure RDTs, ACTs, severe malaria medications, and laboratory supplies and will promote enhanced collaboration and communication between the NDU, NPHRL, the counties, and the NMCP in developing strategies for resource planning, integrated supportive supervision, and development of an external quality assurance system. PMI will work with the NMCP and Global Fund to ensure that the RDT and ACT needs for 2016 and 2017 are met in the NMCP's revised procurement and supply management plan to be submitted during the third quarter of 2015.

Proposed activities with FY 2016 funding: **($4,147,816)**

- Procurement of RDTs. Liberia relies entirely on the Global Fund and PMI to provide RDTs for public facilities and private sector facilities that get their supplies through the NDS and report via the HMIS, as well as iCCM providers. PMI-procured RDTs will help fill any remaining gap or strategically bridge transitions in Global Fund mechanisms and procurements. In FY 2016, PMI will procure 1.4 million RDTs. ($742,000)

- Procure laboratory supplies. PMI will procure quality laboratory supplies, including Giemsa stain, slides, bulbs, and replacement parts for microscopes in health facilities across the country. In addition, PMI will work with the Global Health Security laboratory activities to assure that malaria specimens are included in the specimen transport system to provide reference capability and ensure sufficient clinical material for the national reference laboratory staff to maintain their malaria microscopy skills. Furthermore, reagents and supplies will be procured for the NRL and any new regional reference laboratories to strengthen their ability to conduct quality assurance activities. ($100,000)

- Procure ACTs. PMI will assure continuity of operations by procuring approximately 1 million ACT treatments for the public sector, community case management providers, and private sector facilities in 2017. Based on the Global Fund's planned procurements,

PMI-procured ACTs will be programed to overcome predicted gaps and bridge transitions in Global Fund mechanisms and procurements. ($650,000)

- <u>Procure parenteral medicines to treat severe malaria</u>. PMI will procure parenteral medicines to treat severe malaria. Compared to planned procurements through the Global Fund, PMI will procure a higher proportion of injectable artesunate—as opposed to IM artemether or IV quinine. The procurement is an increase over the amount programmed for FY 2015, but expected to be lower than the expanded PMI procurement scheduled in May 2015. ($140,816)

- <u>Central and facility level capacity development and supportive supervision</u>. As part of a comprehensive approach to malaria case management practices that emphasize testing of all suspected cases and treatment of only positive cases with an ACT, the MOH will continue to support health facilities in updating case management practices based on best practices, and will monitor adherence to policy guidelines.

    o Capacity development and support to the NMCP through a FARA to provide supportive supervision for facility-based health workers in malaria diagnosis and in prompt and appropriate treatment of malaria. This activity will emphasize clinicians adherence to test results, use of case management algorithms, reporting of malaria data to the HMIS, and triangulation of data for decision making. ($550,000)

    o Technical assistance for capacity development and supportive supervision for malaria diagnosis and case management at the central level and in the USAID focus counties of Bong, Lofa, and Nimba. This activity includes support to the NPHRL, NDU, and NMCP to enable effective training and supportive supervision at the county and facility level and supports the training costs for up to ten students to complete laboratory technical certification. ($305,000)

    o Technical assistance for capacity development and supportive supervision for malaria diagnosis and case management in the remaining 12 non-USAID focus counties. ($400,000)

- <u>Capacity development of community-based health workers in prompt and appropriate treatment of malaria and technical assistance for iCCM scale-up.</u>

    o Capacity development and support to the NMCP through a FARA to provide integrated community case management through service delivery partners in USAID focus counties. ($550,000)

    o Technical assistance to expand integrated community case management at the central MOH and in USAID focus counties. At the central level, support for iCCM will entail improving management and stewardship of community health service delivery systems by the MOH, e.g., strengthening the community health services division of the MOH. ($200,000)

46

- o Technical assistance to expand integrated community case management in the remaining 12 non-USAID focus counties. ($300,000)

- Support for strengthening malaria case management and diagnosis in private sector facilities.

  - o Technical assistance to expand malaria diagnosis and treatment at private sector health facilities in USAID focus counties. ($100,000)

  - o Technical assistance to expand malaria diagnosis and treatment at private sector health facilities in the remaining 12 non-USAID focus counties. ($100,000)

- Technical assistance for malaria diagnostics. CDC will provide technical assistance to the NMCP and the NDU/NPHRL for monitoring and improvement of the quality assurance activities for malaria diagnostics at all levels of the health care system, including testing by private facilities, pharmacies, medicine stores, and iCCM. ($10,000)

b. Pharmaceutical Management

NMCP/PMI objectives
The MOH, in collaboration with PMI and other partners, continues to demonstrate commitment to ensuring an effective supply chain system for the distribution of health commodities.

Progress since PMI was launched
A 10-year Supply Chain Master Plan was developed in 2010, integrating all pharmaceutical logistics into a single system to ensure transparency and responsiveness. Though significant progress has been made toward scaling up access to antimalarial drugs and other commodities nationally, and a national LMIS has been established, the national logistics system has continued to face significant challenges such as ensuring full availability of supplies at all levels, and providing accountability over inventory. Following a PMI-supported Supply Logistics Internal Controls Evaluation (SLICE) in 2012 that indicated significant risks of leakage and diversion, the MOH, PMI, and the Global Fund temporarily suspended distribution of donated malaria commodities by the GOL pending the institution of additional controls. In 2013, the MOH, in collaboration with PMI and the Global Fund, piloted an interim approach throughout Liberia using a "top-up" system whereby MOH staff accompany deliveries and verify stock reports from the county level down to the facility level.

Progress during the last 12-18 months
The interim approach was to be evaluated in late 2014; however, due to the Ebola crisis, the evaluation was postponed and both PMI and the Global Fund continued to utilize the system to keep commodities flowing to facilities during the outbreak to the extent possible. The Ebola crisis led to further disruption and fragmentation of the fragile national supply chain, leading to

the establishment of a parallel system for distribution of infection prevention, control, and personal protective equipment commodities.

Monthly stock balance reports continue to be produced by the NDS since the initiation of the interim approach in 2013 with support from PMI, improving the availability of data for planning at the central level. LMIS functioning has deteriorated following implementation of the interim approach due to the inclusion of on-site verification of stock on hand at point of delivery, reducing the incentive to report and penalty for non-compliance. However, the interim approach has provided some useful information for the national quantification exercise for malaria commodities. In early 2015, a national forecast and quantification committee was established and replicated in USAID-focus counties to coordinate forecasting, quantification, and supply planning of malaria commodities both at the county and central levels.

The storage and distribution of malaria commodities remains integrated through a distribution framework involving the disease programs and the essential drugs program of the MOH through the interim approach. The distribution system piloted as part of the interim approach includes commodities for malaria, HIV/AIDS, tuberculosis, reproductive health, and essential drugs. With PMI support, the quantification for essential medicines was conducted and informed a national supply plan for essential medicines. As part of the enhanced government-to-government collaboration through the FARA mechanism, PMI supported the initiation of a uniform storage and distribution system involving harmonized stock status reports of malaria and other health commodities available in the warehouses of the FARA-contracted NGOs in the counties and the county depots as well as a common distribution plan for county-level distribution of health commodities.

Following five nationwide rounds of distribution under the interim approach, monitoring data indicated improvements in visibility, accountability, and availability of health commodities in PMI-supported counties; however, stockouts remained common at all levels of the system. Maintaining the supply chain system remains a challenge to the effective implementation of the Essential Package of Health Services, the cornerstone of Liberia's 10-year National Health Plan. Central to this problem is the assurance of continued funding for warehousing and distribution, as well as local capacity development that will ensure that supervision and management of pharmaceuticals in Liberia is uninterrupted. Equally critical is the development of dedicated county-level supply chain management capacity within county health teams to effectively coordinate the supply planning and distribution of health commodities between NGOs operating in the counties and the NDS, and to monitor stock levels to ensure full availability. Distribution of malaria commodities has improved as a direct outcome of the interim approach.

A 2015 assessment of the interim approach is planned that will provide the GOL and partners the opportunity to analyze the current situation evolving around supply chain management to determine the best option for implementing supply chain activities that ensures the supply chain system in Liberia has adequate infrastructure and systems in place to identify, document, monitor, and report inventory movement and health commodities transactions.

Due to the Ebola epidemic, the supply chain was overstretched as the country was flooded with commodities and limited human resources to manage these commodities. PMI expressed support for an MOH initiative, leveraging other donor financing, to design an outsourcing model for NDS operations via a management contractor to support internal financial management and procurement systems. In 2016, PMI will press for implementation of this model and for completion and operation of the new NDS warehouse jointly financed by PMI and the Global Fund.

The Supply Chain Task Force, involving key supply chain stakeholders and partners, continues its routine meetings to address emerging problems of the supply chain system in a timely and concerted manner, providing another venue for enhanced coordination and support to the MOH for effective supply chain management that supports routine health services and emergency response.

Plans and justification

In 2016, PMI will support the implementation of the agreed-upon approach by the MOH for supply planning and distribution of health commodities, in collaboration with the SCMU and the Global Fund. PMI's continued support to the supply chain system will be critical in order for the MOH to move away from the interim approach system and settle for a more sustainable and institutionalized system for facility-level distribution. The establishment of county-level supply chain management capacity within the CHTs to coordinate supply planning and distribution of health commodities at the county-level will remain crucial to ensure health commodities are accounted for, available, and secure from the central level to the health facilities. This will continue to be evaluated through routine monitoring and reporting, and the periodic conduct of end-use verification (EUV) surveys. PMI will also support system-wide efforts to evaluate, redesign, and roll out a revised supply chain distribution system following the interim approach, and a revised LMIS system aimed at providing more reliable routine reporting data than is currently available.

Proposed activities with FY 2016 funding: **($1,150,000)**

- Support the implementation and rollout of the revised LMIS and improve the availability and use of consumption data at both the county and facility levels. ($100,000)

- Strengthen supply chain management (central level). Support the operations of a new NDS warehouse, provide mentoring to the SCMU, and improve supervision, forecasting, and quantification nationally and in accordance with the revised supply chain master plan. ($450,000)

- Strengthen supply chain management (county/district). Expand support to county depots and CHTs in Bong, Nimba, Margibi, and Montserrado counties to rationalize commodity management, storage, supervision of commodity distribution, and reporting in line with the revised supply chain master plan. ($400,000)

- Monitor antimalarial drug quality. Continue support to the LMHRA, Pharmacy Board, and the MOH systems to strengthen the regulatory environment for pharmaceutical management through routine monitoring of antimalarial drug quality and quality assurance. ($150,000)

- Regulation and rational use of pharmaceuticals. Provide technical assistance to the LMHRA, Pharmacy Board, and MOH systems to strengthen the policy environment for drug regulation and rational use of pharmaceuticals. ($50,000)

5. Health system strengthening and capacity building

PMI supports a broad array of health system strengthening activities which cut across intervention areas, such as strengthening in-service training of health workers, supply chain management, health information systems, regulation of health services and pharmaceuticals, and capacity-building of the NMCP as well as that of County Health Teams and supervisors to monitor and improve the quality of malaria interventions in the health system. In addition, PMI provides a portion of its support for malaria service delivery and quality improvement directly to the GOL through USAID's FARA with the Ministry of Health, while supporting technical assistance and capacity building of MOH systems to utilize FARA resources to improve the delivery of malaria services.

NMCP/PMI objectives
A high priority of the NMCP is to increase the qualifications of its staff, particularly in terms of their managerial and supervisory capacity. In addition, the Liberia MOH has made a commitment to decentralize services to the county level and to integrate health services at both the health facility and the community level in order to improve access to health care. Strengthening the capacity of lower levels of the health care system management, particularly at the level of County and District Health Teams, to manage, supervise, and improve the quality of malaria services and program implementation is also a key priority.

Progress since PMI was launched
To encourage integration of malaria prevention and control activities into routine health care in ways that are sustainable, PMI has supported the NMCP to more actively engage with other parts of the MOH involved in malaria-related activities, such as the Reproductive Health Division, Community Health Division, Maternal and Child Health Division, the NDU, regulatory bodies and professional associations such as the Liberia Medical and Dental Council and the Liberia Medicines and Health Products Regulatory Authority (LHMRA), and county health teams and supervisors.

As part of the transition to a decentralized system, NMCP staff members are adapting to their changing roles in terms of integrated supervision, policy implementation, advocacy, and mentoring of staff on CHTs. Instead of directly providing services, the NMCP is now charged with ensuring that malaria prevention and control measures are well conducted and policy changes are implemented. Parallel to this change is the expansion of the HMIS data system to include more facilities, making it a more representative and useful data tool. The NMCP now also participates as part of the FARA management committee.

PMI support from 2008 to 2014 to build the capacity of the NMCP and counties for management of service delivery has helped to achieve substantial improvements in the capacity and reach of the health system, particularly at the local level. In FY 2014, USAID assisted the MOH to conduct capacity self-assessments of internal MOH and county-level systems and supporting services looking at functions in each of six WHO Health System Building Blocks, as a follow-up to baseline assessments conducted two years earlier just after the FARA activity was initiated. Quantitative capacity scores for the central MOH increased from a baseline of 59% in 2012 to 79% in 2014, and scores at the county level increased from an average of 44% to 78% in Bong, Lofa and Nimba. Qualitative findings highlighted variability across counties and operating units, but also substantial progress in most system functions.

Progress during the last 12-18 months
Despite the Ebola outbreak, PMI investments have helped to sustain progress over the past 12-18 months toward development of MOH systems and functions to support malaria services, including supply chain, in-service training of health workers, support for quality improvement and quality assurance, and development of health information systems.

PMI Resident Advisors provided direct support and mentoring to the NMCP, and PMI supported implementation of Liberia's Global Fund malaria grant through a long-term technical advisor based in the NMCP. An organizational assessment of the NMCP resulted in a revised organogram, organizational terms of reference, and a staffing plan with job descriptions in response to Global Fund grant conditions. PMI also provided additional technical assistance to support coordination and planning of the ongoing universal coverage campaign of Global Fund-procured bed nets and supported light renovations of NMCP offices to facilitate part-time co-location for PMI advisors.

In supply chain, continued PMI support for the interim approach helped to enhance visibility and accountability for both GOL and donated products, and ensured that malaria products continued to flow to service delivery points even during the Ebola outbreak. In PMI focus counties, stockouts of adult malaria medications (AS/AQ) went from 93% at the start of the first round in October 2013 to 35% following the third round in mid-2014 – still unacceptably high, but an enormous achievement. The system needs to be evaluated and will be redesigned in the coming year to improve efficiency and further improve continuous availability of products including LLINs for routine distribution.

PMI support to improve the quality and utilization of data continued through 2014, with a focus on improving the use of DHIS2 at the county level. A follow-up Performance of Routine Health Information Systems assessment indicating the accuracy of facility data had increased from 55% to 84% since a 2012 baseline assessment, and completeness improved from 52% to 79%. In order to increase staff skills in data analysis and interpretation at the central level, PMI and the Global Fund also sponsored three MOH/NMCP staff to participate in a regional M&E training in Ghana. A PMI-supported insectary was established and continued to operate at the NMCP to support entomological monitoring, and NMCP sampling activities continued even through the Ebola outbreak.

Under the FARA, a reimbursement agreement with the MOH for health services delivery supported by PMI and other USAID funding, the MOH continued to contract out with NGOs in Bong, Nimba, and Lofa counties to support service delivery and provide technical assistance for health system functioning in over 120 facilities. The NMCP participated in the management of FARA activities, as well as the production of key FARA deliverables such as joint integrated supportive supervision reports. The NMCP also participated in the integrated supportive supervision of health facilities; a key activity supported by the FARA in Bong, Lofa, and Nimba and supported by other donors in Liberia's other 12 counties. PMI provided technical assistance and support to the MOH to implement the FARA at all levels through strengthening of supervision systems and processes, support to improve management, HMIS and data use, and introduction of quality assurance and quality control mechanisms at all levels.

The disruption in malaria services due to Ebola was significant, leaving many facilities and services operating at a lower level at the time of the MOP writing than one year prior. During the height of the crisis, less than half of Liberia's health facilities were seeing patients, and many others were providing only limited services. PMI worked to quickly adapt programs to the unfolding situation, and advise the GOL in adjusting technical approaches to sustain access to malaria services and protect health workers – such as by shifting temporarily to a "no-touch" approach to treatment of malaria and other common illnesses by using presumptive treatment in settings without adequate protective equipment, in line with WHO recommendations. PMI also shifted commodity procurements in response to a drop in consumption of RDTs and increased consumption of ACTs to avoid wastage, and helped to ensure malaria products continued to be distributed through the crisis. PMI is also now playing an important role in supporting restoration of health service delivery by accelerating efforts to expand coverage of malaria interventions.

Plans and justification
PMI will continue its strong focus on building technical and managerial capacity for malaria prevention and control at all levels of the health care system, including support for decentralization of management and oversight capacity to the county and district levels in line with GOL policy. This is built into PMI's overall approach of supporting the MOH directly to improve delivery of malaria service in targeted counties, combined with support and technical assistance to the central MOH to strengthen health system functions at the national level. A key shift is that in FY 2016, PMI will continue to focus county-level interventions on the USG's three focus counties, but also provide additional technical assistance to the MOH to ensure malaria interventions are strengthened in Liberia's other 12 counties, thus leveraging other donor and GOL resources.

PMI will continue to support the NMCP to improve the quality, completeness, and timeliness of malaria-specific data reporting from health facilities, surveys, and supervision, and to increase staff skills in data analysis and interpretation. PMI will continue to support distribution and management of malaria commodities as well as broader strengthening of the supply chain system, including support to implement a redesigned national supply chain master plan to be developed in the coming year with PMI support. PMI will also continue support for entomological monitoring, with NMCP staff playing the lead role in continued operation of the insectary, as well as support to the LMHRA to expand drug quality surveillance and regulation. PMI will also place an increased emphasis on supporting quality assurance/quality improvement of facility-based malaria services, improved regulation of pharmaceuticals, roll-out of enhanced supervision and service delivery protocols, and scale-up and revitalization of community-based interventions including iCCM.

Although no PMI funds will be going to support CDC's Field Epidemiology and LaboratoryTraining Program, as part of the response to EVD and development of a resilient health system, CDC is supporting a shortened (3 month) course for approximately 125 monitoring and evaluation officers at the national, county, and district levels over the next two years. National monitoring and evaluation staff from the NMCP are slated to be included in this training and will benefit from the training of the county and district health teams.

Proposed activities with FY 2016 funding: **($580,000)**

NMCP capacity building
- Long-term technical assistance to strengthen management, leadership and planning capacity of NMCP. Liberia has had a favorable experience with the long-term technical assistance recently inaugurated through PMI for assistance with implementation of Global Fund activities; therefore, PMI will continue to support this technical assistance in the form of mentoring to sustain/further improveme the NMCP's management and oversight, both internally (e.g., meeting efficiency, setting timelines, achieving milestones) and externally (e.g., donor and implementing partner coordination). A second technical assistance position will also be established to allow for increased support outside the NMCP in terms of relations with other segments of the MOH and for supportive supervision with the CHTs ($450,000).

- Support for strengthening NMCP and CHT capacity for program management. To complement the internal mentoring of staff within the NMCP described above, efforts to strengthen the entire MOH (e.g., Family Health and Community Services Divisions) will targeted support to assure comprehensive and up-to-date malaria content (e.g., integrated post-training follow-up of health workers), and will address specific linkages with the NMCP including integrated supervision, particularly in the follow-up of issues identified to achieve solutions prior to the next round of integrated supervision. ($130,000)

Table 9: Health Systems Strengthening Activities

HSS Building Block	Technical Area	Description of Activity
Health Services	Case Management	Improve, through training and supervision, QA systems to monitor the quality of laboratory diagnostic services.
Health Workforce	Health Systems Strengthening	Build, through training and technical assistance, host country managerial and leadership capacity for effective malaria control
Health Information	Monitoring and Evaluation	Participate in post-EVD strengthening of disease surveillance systems to improve decision-making, planning, forecasting, and program management
		Support revision and implementation of an updated LMIS
		Support monitoring of commodity availability at health facilities through EUV surveys
Essential Medical Products, Vaccines, and Technologies	Case Management	Support improved forecasting, procurement, quality control, storage and distribution of malaria commodities, such as insecticide-treated nets, artemisinin-based combination therapies and rapid diagnostic tests.
		Strengthen the regulatory environment for pharmaceutical management and routine monitoring of drug quality
Leadership and Governance	Health Systems Strengthening	Strengthen NMCP and national coordinating and regulatory bodies to direct and manage malaria resources, develop guidelines, and improve quality of services.

6. Behavior change communication

NMCP/PMI objectives
Liberia's 2016-2020 National Malaria Strategic Plan is being finalized and plans are underway to revise the 2005 Malaria BCC Community Strategy. The current BCC strategy focuses on the dissemination of malaria-related messaging through mass media, interpersonal communication, and community engagement activities to help ensure that children under five years of age receive effective ACT treatment within 24 hours, that pregnant women receive at least three doses of IPTp, and that community members are aware of the benefits of and are using LLINs to prevent malaria. The current national malaria health promotion targets include the following:

- 90% of the population has heard a malaria message through multimedia channels
- 80% of community health committees and local leaders are reached with advocacy activities

- 100% of legislators and county superintendents are provided with information on malaria prevention, control, and treatment strategies

Progress since PMI was launched
Concerted efforts from PMI and the Global Fund have successfully raised the population's awareness of malaria. The 2011 MIS indicated that 97% of women of reproductive age have heard of malaria and, of those, 82% cited mosquitoes as the cause of malaria. Moreover, among those women who have heard of malaria and who say there are ways to avoid getting malaria or that malaria can be treated, 80% of women cited use of mosquito nets as a way to avoid infection, and 61% knew to treat malaria with ACTs.

In late 2013, the NMCP established a malaria BCC technical working group at the national/central level. This working group, which is progressively becoming operational, will focus on technical issues related to malaria BCC strategy development, materials/messaging, medium of conveying messages, appropriate target audiences, timing, M&E of BCC activities, and BCC community outreach.

Progress during the last 12-18 months
In 2014, PMI provided support for a strategic behavior change communication survey in four counties (Bong, Grand Cape Mount, Grand Kru, and River Cess counties) to examine attitudes, beliefs and practices regarding net use, receipt of ACTs by children with fever, IPTp for pregnant women, and to identify communication gaps associated with current malaria BCC messaging.[8] Similar to the 2011 MIS results, most participants had heard of malaria, were familiar with its symptoms, and mentioned mosquito nets as a prevention method. Nevertheless, only 41% of the participants in the 2014 survey were found to have adequate knowledge about malaria prevention (defined as mentioning at least one correct prevention method and no incorrect prevention methods). In terms of exposure to BCC messaging, while only 42% of the participants in the 2011 MIS reported having seen or heard a malaria message in the past few months, 82% of the 2014 BCC survey participants recalled having heard or seen a malaria message within the past 12 months. Despite this, only 19% of the BCC survey respondents were able to correctly identify key messages from the "Healthy Baby, Happy Mother" campaign which was focused on improving care seeking for fever among children less than five years of age. Additional findings from the 2014 survey indicate a disparity in malaria-related knowledge across the four study counties and a need for improvements in malaria BCC messaging and dissemination for IPTp specifically and malaria in general. Summary findings from the 2014 BCC survey appear in the table below. The results of this survey are being taken into account in the revision of the national BCC strategy, specifically in terms of increasing knowledge of pregnant women with regards to IPTp.

---

[8] Health Communication Capacity Collaborative. Attitudes, Beliefs and Practices Relevant to Malaria Prevention and Treatment in Liberia, 2014. The study was conducted in four counties (Bong, Grand Cape Mount, Grand Kru, River Cess) and included a total of 1200 women and 360 men from households where a child under five years of age resided.

Table 10: Summary findings from the 2014 strategic behavior change communication survey in Bong, Grand Cape Mount, Grand Kru, and River Cess counties, N=1,560

	Overall	Bong	Grand Cape Mount	Grand Kru	River Cess
General Knowledge and Beliefs About Malaria and Malaria Prevention					
% who mentioned mosquitoes as a cause of malaria	93	93	93	87	99
% who mentioned fever as a primary symptom of malaria	52	75	35	40	58
% with adequate malaria prevention knowledge (mentioned at least one correct prevention method and no incorrect prevention methods)	41	28	47	37	50
% who believe nets are effective at preventing malaria	26	26	21	29	29
General Knowledge and Beliefs About ANC and IPTp					
% who believe that at least half of women in their community complete four or more ANC visits during pregnancy	57	70	68	19	70
% who mentioned SP as drug used to prevent malaria in pregnancy	53	67	39	38	67
% who knew when IPTp should be started during pregnancy	11	5	2	8	30
% who believe IPTp is effective in preventing malaria during pregnancy	12	11	10	4	22
General Beliefs about Malaria Diagnosis and Treatment					
% who believed malaria test was effective at diagnosing malaria	49	51	17	61	67
% who had positive attitudes towards malaria treatment	43	42	14	57	59
% who believe at least half of children in their community visit a health provider the same or next day they develop a fever	56	71	75	7	69
Exposure to Health Messages					
% who listen to radio at least once per week	60	59	52	51	79
% who recall hearing or seeing a message about malaria prevention or treatment within the last 12 months	82	88	72	70	97
% who recall hearing or seeing the phrase "Take Cover Under the Net" during the last six months	75	80	73	52	94
% who recall hearing or seeing the phrase "Healthy Baby, Happy Mother" during the	74	82	76	48	90

last 12 months					
% who correctly identified key messages of the "Healthy Baby, Happy Mother Campaign"	19	42	3	11	16

Malaria BCC activities are part of Liberia's integrated basic health service delivery package. Over the past year, PMI and its implementing partners continued to assist the MOH in developing communication materials, as well as training and equipping health providers, including gCHVs, to convey malaria messages. A 26-part serial drama, "Baby by Choice, Not by Chance," included malaria prevention and treatment messages. The drama was broadcast on seven community radio stations and one Monrovia-based radio station from September 2013 to February 2014. In addition, the revised MIP guidelines were validated in November 2014 and finalization of MIP messages and materials based on the revised guidelines is currently underway.

Liberia's EVD epidemic, which started in March 2014, had a negative impact on the NMCP's BCC activities in that the MOH initially placed a moratorium on all non Ebola-related activities. EVD messaging initially took priority over malaria messages in the media and some of the PMI-supported malaria BCC activities were delayed. Despite these challenges, PMI and its implementing partners provided support for the development and dissemination of BCC messaging for the April 2015 national LLIN campaign and for the development of a post-EVD malaria transition plan. Based on the EVD community engagement strategy, the plan will use existing community structures and gCHVs to disseminate malaria messaging through drama groups and community outreach sessions.

Plans and justification

In addition to advocating for more interpersonal communication versus mass media to address the issue of translating knowledge into behavior change, the NMCP has identified the need for greater continuity in malaria messaging. To date, malaria messaging has primarily been driven by specific campaigns. The revised national BCC strategy will include a focus on engaging national and local media on malaria topics on a regular basis and greater media participation in malaria-related events, and will include updated language regarding universal testing prior to malaria treatment, including in the private sector. PMI will provide continued support for the revision of the national BCC strategy and related materials and the development of tools to strengthen the interpersonal communication skills of health providers. Meanwhile, mass media will continue to be used and reinforced to concomitantly maintain and sustain acquired knowledge and boost behavior change on all malaria interventions promoted by PMI in Liberia.

The impact of PMI's contribution to behavior change in Liberia will be measured through the monitoring of BCC interventions, using the HMIS to monitor improved intervention uptake, and with the next MIS, which is planned for 2016.

Proposed activities with FY 2016 funding: ($1,000,000)

- Integrated interpersonal communication and BCC. PMI will support the continued implementation of integrated interpersonal communication in Bong, Lofa, Nimba, Margibi, and Montserrado counties to promote all aspects of malaria interventions. These counties account for approximately 70% of the population of Liberia. Health providers, including gCHVs, will be trained on how to effectively communicate preventive and curative messages to mothers/caretakers. ($400,000)

- <u>Support for BCC through community health services interventions/interpersonal communication, mass media communications.</u> PMI will support the development and dissemination of BCC messaging for all malaria interventions including a focus on BCC for LLINs, iCCM, IPTp, and testing prior to treatment in the private sector. Messages will be in local languages and tailored for various locations/groups.

    o At the central level and in Bong, Nimba, and Lofa counties. ($200,000)
    o In Liberia's 12 non-USAID focus counties. ($400,000)

7. Monitoring and evaluation

NMCP/PMI Objectives
Liberia's National Malaria Strategic Plan 2010–2015 calls for monitoring the progress toward program goals and evaluation of the impact and outcomes of planned interventions. Additionally, the plan calls for the implementation of evidence-based program management. The NMCP's 2010–2015 M&E plan uses facility- and population-based indicators consistent with global standards and is fully costed. The NMCP is currently updating the Malaria Strategic Plan 2016–2020 and accompanying costed M&E plan. The new draft objective is by 2020, to increase to 90% reporting structures (health facilities, private pharmacies & medicine stores and communities) that provide quality and complete malaria data to measure progress and provide evidence. Monitoring and evaluation activities take place at all levels of the health care system and are conducted by the NMCP in collaboration with the Central Monitoring and Evaluation Unit of the MOH. Coordination occurs through quarterly M&E Technical Working Group meetings.

PMI's support to M&E in Liberia aligns with the NMCP's M&E plan. Sources of data and information will include the routine health information system, periodic household and facility surveys, and activity reports from the implementing partners.

Progress since PMI was launched
PMI and the Global Fund have provided the bulk of the funding for M&E activities in Liberia over the past several years. PMI has supported two MIS surveys (MIS 2009 and MIS 2011) to track the coverage of malaria interventions and malaria parasitemia and contributed to one DHS (DHS 2013). PMI has been supporting the end-use verification (EUV) surveys to assess the availability of malaria commodities at health facilities since 2010. PMI, along with Global Fund, has also provided continuing support for the NMCP to conduct supportive supervision activities to strengthen data collection and reporting through the Health Management Information System (HMIS) at the health facilities through the county level and finally to the national level. PMI supported sentinel sites up until 2010 to track trends in malaria morbidity and mortality. Global Fund support will be used to establish new sentinel sites (one per region). Two sentinel sites were established in 2015, with plans to add three more by the end of 2015. In this context sentinel sites refers to special support to facilities to improve their ability to report via the DHIS.

The data collected is at the aggregate level (e.g., total number tested and total positives treated for malaria).

Progress during the last 12–18 months
The 2013 DHS report was released in 2014. The survey was powered to provide data at the county level for questions asked of all participants. The results are provided in the Progress on Indicators to Date section.

The MOH has a fully integrated computerized HMIS based on data collected manually from health facilities through the CHTs that serves all departments (including inpatient) and programs, including malaria care and treatment and distribution of nets at ANC visits and institutional deliveries. Personnel at all levels have been trained and the system is operational nationwide. Private health care facilities (including some private pharmacies and medicines stores) that receive commodities and support from the government and provide malaria diagnostic services, medications, and case management are also expected to report. Approximately 210 private facilities treated and reported on malaria as of 2014. The HMIS currently does not yet collect data from gCHVs. In 2013, the MOH with support from PMI and USAID began designing a community health information system (C-HMIS) that will be integrated with the current facility-based HMIS. These community level registers were distributed in 2013 but have not yet been uniformly utilized, and the C-HMIS module is not incorporated into DHIS2 yet. The Ebola crisis resulted in delays in implementing C-HMIS, though it has now emerged as a priority for post-Ebola health service restoration.

PMI supported technical assistance for CHT (County Health Team) M&E officers to conduct regular monitoring of reported data in DHIS2 for treatment for malaria at community and facility levels and IPTp.

PMI contributed to the MOH's review of the HMIS system in March 2014. The process included a review of the indicators and the design and printing of revised recording and reporting instruments. The first step in the review process was to review the national list of indicators with each division, including the NMCP, and data users at central and county levels. Indicators were revised, added, or dropped based on these discussions. In April 2014, a national stakeholder meeting was convened where the revised list of indicators was presented to all users to provide feedback. The second step in the process was to review the current HMIS reporting and recording forms in light of the revised list of indicators. As a result of this review, new registers, including a revised monthly reporting form, were designed to better capture the data. Due to the Ebola crisis, the new registers have not been rolled out.

An assessment of the overall routine HMIS system was conducted in 2012 in Bong, Lofa, Nimba, and Grand Bassa counties using the Performance of Routine Information System Management framework and tools. A follow-up assessment supported by PMI in 2014 showed data quality and use has improved since 2012 at the county and health facility level. For example, data accuracy in the HMIS at the facility level improved from 55% in 2012 to 84% in 2014.[9]

---

[9] Liberia Rebuilding Health Services Year 6 Annual Report. 2014.

In partnership with the NMCP and the SCMU, PMI has supported EUV surveys since 2010. The EUV is a rapid survey that collects data from a sample of health facilities each quarter on the availability of malaria commodities. The survey takes eight weeks from facility visits to the production of the final report and includes a follow-up plan to correct any problems found. Follow-up actions have included emergency procurements, training of health workers, and facilitating requisitions. The latest EUV survey in January 2015 was being combined with data collection for verification of the implementation of the "interim approach" for the supply chain since the reporting needs overlapped. This EUV survey indicated that 12–19% of health facilities were stocked out of AS/AQ, depending on the presentation, 39% were stocked out of RDTs and 33% were stocked out of SP.[10]

Despite a sound M&E vision, the MOH and NMCP have had problems implementing their routine systems, such as the HMIS, because of limited technical capacity, funding, oversight, and turnover of health facility staff. This has resulted in issues with the quality, timeliness, and completeness of the data, and the system is still primarily used for the creation of required reports and underutilized for surveillance, supportive supervision, monitoring, and planning. PMI is continuing to provide support to strengthen the collection, reporting, and use of HMIS data. The DHIS software is available and M&E staff members are in place in all county health offices, both of which present opportunities for improving the quality and use of data reported through the HMIS system.

Two assessments of the HMIS were conducted in 2012 and 2014 utilizing the PRISM tool.[11] For the June 2014 assessment, data collection in the field was conducted in four of the 15 counties (Bong, Nimba, Lofa, and Grand Bassa counties). All of the four county health offices and a random sample of 76 health facilities (19 health facilities per county) were surveyed, and about 283 health managers and staff from these institutions were interviewed. Overall accuracy at the facilities improved from 55% to 84%, and data completeness in facilities' monthly reports improved from 52% to 79%. Completeness of monthly reports at the county level was 91% in 2012 and 98% in 2014. Timeliness of reports of health facilities at county levels rose from 74% in 2012 to 88% in 2014. Note that the 2014 assessment does not capture the effects of EVD. Reporting dipped significantly through November last year but is recovering, as is the entire health system. Reporting is a key portion of a resilient health system thus there are a variety of partners, particularly USAID and World Bank, who are working specifically on improving reporting at the macro level (e.g., enhanced internet capacity) all the way to the data entry person.

The table below summarizes the available data sources and assessments since 2010 and planned activities through 2018.

[10] PMI End-Use Verification Liberia January 2015. USAID/DELIVER Project.
[11] Liberia Rebuilding Health Services Year 6 Annual Report. 2014.

Table 11: Monitoring and Evaluation Data Sources in Liberia, 2010–2018

Data Source	Survey Activities	Year								
		2010	2011	2012	2013	2014	2015	2016	2017	2018
National-level Household surveys	Demographic Health Survey (DHS)				X					
	Malaria Indicator Survey (MIS)		X					(X)		
	National census									(X)*
Health Facility and Other Surveys	Health Facility Survey				X*		(X)*			
	HMIS assessment--PRISM[a]			X		X				
	EUV survey	X	X	X	X	X	X	(X)	(X)	(X)
	ITN Post-campaign Survey						(X)			
Malaria Surveillance and Routine System Support	Support to HMIS/DHIS2	X	X	X	X	X	X	(X)	(X)	(X)
	Sentinel surveillance sites	X					X*	(X)*	(X)*	(X)*
Therapeutic Efficacy monitoring	*In vivo* efficacy testing						(X)*		(X)	
Entomology	Entomological surveillance and resistance monitoring	X	X	X	X	X	X	(X)	(X)	(X)
Other malaria-related evaluations	Malaria Program Review/Midterm Review					X*				
Other Data Sources	Malaria Impact Evaluation						X	(X)		

*Not PMI-funded
[a]Performance of Routine Information System Management—Bong, Lofa, Nimba, Grand Bassa counties

Plans and justification
The NMCP M&E plan is integrated and financed by three sources: PMI, the Global Fund, and the GOL. PMI support to the NMCP's M&E strategy complements Global Fund support and will help provide key population-based indicators for monitoring malaria program implementation. PMI supports population-based surveys such as the DHS and MIS and provides technical assistance with the HMIS. PMI also supports data quality assurance and supportive supervision

through the FARA with the MOH, while the Global Fund provides funding to support facility data, such as HMIS, health facility surveys, and supportive supervision for data quality assurance. Funding through the Global Fund will also be used to establish up to five sentinel sites for collecting epidemiologic data on malaria. PMI and Global Fund resources will support therapeutic efficacy studies with Global Fund supporting 2015 activities and PMI support planned for 2017.

Improving HMIS data reporting and use will be addressed jointly with the Global Fund and will focus on enhancing the NMCP's capacity to supervise and support counties and districts in their malaria specific M&E activities. PMI funding will support follow-up activities resulting from the 2014 HMIS assessment.

Proposed activities with FY 2016 funding: **($920,000)**

- <u>Strengthening data collection and dissemination for decision making (national level)</u>. The goal of this activity is to improve the collection, reporting, and use of various sources of data including household survey data, HMIS data, implementing partner data, and health facility survey data for decision-making at the national level by the MOH. Support will also be provided to strengthen malaria reporting in DHIS2 and to improve translation of HMIS data to strengthen malaria programming at the central level. ($200,000)

- <u>Strengthen data collection and use (county level)</u>. This activity will support the collection, reporting, and use of malaria data through the HMIS system at the county level in Bong, Lofa, and Nimba counties. There is a need for the county health teams to analyze the monthly HMIS data and use it to track trends in malaria indicators and properly respond. This funding will contribute to the planned embedded technical assistance in the county health teams to ensure that malaria cases and deaths are properly tracked from the health facility level to the county level and to support the county health team to analyze and use the data on malaria trends in responding to changes in the number of malaria cases and planning commodity needs. This activity will also link with the recording of community data from gCHVs and private sector data as separate entries until they are incorporated in the HMIS system (e.g. C-HMIS) and will ensure health facilities are using the proper registers to record patient data. ($100,000)

- <u>Strengthen data collection and use (county level)</u>. This activity will support the collection, reporting, and use of malaria data through the HMIS system at the county level. Resources will be provided for technical assistance and to support visits by the MOH and NMCP to the remaining 12 counties, which are, with the exception of Montserrado where the MOH is located, much less populated, at which lessons learned from the three counties above will be shared with the respective county health teams as part of on-site supportive supervision. ($200,000)

- <u>PMI will provide support for the malaria module in the 2019 DHS</u>. Liberia has a census planned for 2018, which will inform the sampling of the 2019 DHS. PMI will support the malaria module in the 2019 DHS. ($200,000)

- End-use verification (EUV) survey. PMI will provide resources to implement the EUV survey on a quarterly basis. Emphasis will be placed on sustainability in terms of simplification of reports, dissemination of results, and follow-up action for any problems identified. ($100,000)

- Therapeutic efficacy monitoring. Support *in vivo* drug efficacy monitoring of first-line antimalarials in two sites, complementing therapeutic efficacy monitoring conducted with Global Fund support. ($100,000)

- Technical Assistance. CDC will conduct two technical assistance visits to support the NMCP on M&E activities. ($20,000)

8. Operational research

NMCP/PMI Objectives

The NMCP Research, Monitoring, and Evaluation Department is responsible for planning and conducting operational research studies in collaboration with other NMCP focal points and partners. An overarching strategic objective for the NMCP is to contribute to the knowledge of malaria epidemiology and control in coastal West Africa through operational research in partnership with higher educational institutions in Liberia. Outside of PMI-funded operational research, the MENTOR Initiative is currently conducting a durable wall lining study in Bomi County, and previously conducted a pilot in greater Monrovia to provide ACTs to private sector pharmacies, along with RDTs for testing.

Progress since PMI was launched
Liberia had one PMI-funded OR study that was completed in 2013 and does not have any ongoing studies or studies planned with FY 2016 funding.

Summary of dried blood tube sample (DTS) OR study

RDTs are currently being scaled up in Liberia. In 2012, CDC/PMI developed a dried blood tube sample (DTS) method that showed potential for use as a stable source of quality control samples to use in an external quality assurance system with RDTs. In order to assess the feasibility of using DTS in field settings, PMI, in conjunction with NMCPs, conducted pilot studies in Liberia and Ethiopia in 2013. The fieldwork in Liberia was conducted from June to December 2013 at the National Drug Quality Control Laboratory and two health facilities. Staff from the NMCP performed the tests at week zero and then every four weeks for six months. Health facility staff were trained to use the DTS and were asked to test a four-sample proficiency panel at 12 and 24 weeks. Preliminary analysis of the data was done in March 2014 and suggested DTS stability in Liberia appears to be affected by prolonged storage under ambient conditions, whereas there was no difference in Ethiopia. A near-final report has been shared with the CDC-PMI Resident Advisor. When finalized, the report will be shared with the NMCP and NDU/NRL. Data from this study and a similar study conducted in Benin will be combined into a single manuscript for publication in a peer-reviewed journal.

Completed OR Studies			
Title	Start date	End date	Budget
Field Testing of Dried Malaria-Positive Blood as Quality Control Samples for Malaria RDTs.	June 2013	December 2013	$10,895*

*Additionally, a MOP-funded TDY was used to support diagnostics, as well as for training and setting up this activity.

Plans and justification
There are no PMI-supported operational research activities planned with FY 2016 funding.

Proposed activities with FY 2016 funding: **($0)**
There are no PMI-supported operational research activities planned with FY 2016 funding.

9. Staffing and administration

Two health professionals serve as resident advisors to oversee PMI in Liberia, one representing CDC and one representing USAID. In addition, one or more Foreign Service Nationals (FSNs) work as part of the PMI team. All PMI staff members are part of a single interagency team led by the USAID Mission Director or his/her designee in country. The PMI team shares responsibility for development and implementation of PMI strategies and work plans, coordination with national authorities, managing collaborating agencies, and supervising day-to-day activities. Candidates for resident advisor positions (whether initial hires or replacements) will be evaluated and/or interviewed jointly by USAID and CDC, and both agencies will be involved in hiring decisions, with the final decision made by the individual agency.

The PMI professional staff work together to oversee all technical and administrative aspects of PMI, including finalizing details of the project design, implementing malaria prevention and treatment activities, monitoring and evaluation of outcomes and impact, reporting of results, and providing guidance to PMI partners.

The PMI lead in country is the USAID Mission Director. The day-to-day lead for PMI is delegated to the USAID Health Office Director and thus the two PMI resident advisors, one from USAID and one from CDC, report to the USAID Health Office Director for day-to-day leadership, and work together as a part of a single interagency team. The technical expertise housed in Atlanta and Washington guides PMI programmatic efforts.

The two PMI resident advisors are based within the USAID health office and are expected to spend approximately half their time sitting with and providing technical assistance to the national malaria control programs and partners.

Locally-hired staff to support PMI activities either in Ministries or in USAID will be approved by the USAID Mission Director. Because of the need to adhere to specific country policies and USAID accounting regulations, any transfer of PMI funds directly to Ministries or host governments will need to be approved by the USAID Mission Director and Controller, in addition to the US Global Malaria Coordinator.

Proposed activities with FY 2016 funding: **($1,051,184)**

- In-country staffing and administration. Coordination and staff salaries and benefits, office equipment and supplies, and routine expenses for PMI activities in Liberia.
  - CDC resident advisor staffing and administration costs ($488,184)
  - USAID resident advisor, FSN(s) and USAID/Liberia Mission-wide costs ($563,000)

Table 1: Budget Breakdown by Mechanism
President's Malaria Initiative – Liberia
Planned Malaria Obligations for FY 2016

Mechanism	Geographic Area	Activity	Budget ($)	%
CDC	Nationwide	Technical assistance for M&E, malaria diagnostics, and vector control	59,000	0.5%
CDC/USAID	Nationwide	In-country staffing and administration	1,051,184	8.8%
CSH	Central, Bong, Lofa, Nimba	Improve quality of care and adherence to standards for MIP; support monitoring and strengthening of diagnostics QA/QC system; support strengthening malaria case management; support use of consumption data at county and facility level; strengthening pharmaceutical regulation and NMCP and CHT capacity for program management; strengthening data collection and use at the central and county levels; end-use verification	1,185,000	9.9%
FARA	Central, Bong, Lofa, Nimba	Capacity development and supportive supervision for malaria diagnostics, in-service supervision and training at ANC facilities, capacity development of facility based and community-based health workers in malaria treatment, interpersonal BCC	1,950,000	16.3%
IRS TO6	Nationwide	Increase NMCP entomology capacity and entomological monitoring	500,000	4.2%
PACS	Central, Bong, Lofa, Nimba	Technical assistance for iCCM scale-up and support for BCC	400,000	3.3%
PQM	Nationwide	Monitoring of antimalarial drug quality	150,000	1.3%
TBD	Nationwide	Technical assistance to strengthen NMCP; DHS 2019; therapeutic efficacy monitoring	750,000	6.3%
TBD - Supply Chain Contract	Nationwide	Procurement of LLINs, ACTs, severe malaria drugs, RDTs, and laboratory supplies; distribution of LLINs; supply chain management support	3,954,816	33.0%

TBD – Technical assistance for non-focus counties	12 non-USAID focus counties	Improve quality of care and adherence to standards for MIP; support monitoring and strengthening of diagnostics QA/QC system and malaria case management; support iCCM scale-up and strengthening malaria case management in the private sector; support for BCC; strengthening data collection and use at the county level	1,600,000	13.3%
VectorWorks	Nationwide	Technical assistance for continuous distribution and 2018 mass campaign planning	400,000	3.3%
Total			**12,000,000**	**100%**

Table 2: Budget Breakdown by Activity
President's Malaria Initiative – Liberia
Planned Malaria Obligations for FY 2016

Proposed Activity	Mechanism	Budget		Geographical area	Description
		Total $	Commodity $		
PREVENTIVE ACTIVITIES					
Insecticide Treated Nets					
Procure LLINs	TBD-Supply Chain Contract	1,152,000	1,152,000	Nationwide	Procure about 320,000 LLINs for routine distribution (ANC and institutional delivery)
Distribute LLINs	TBD-Supply Chain Contract	320,000		Nationwide	LLIN distribution (including warehousing and transportation down to facility level at an average cost of $1 per net)
Technical assistance for continuous distribution and technical assistance for 2018 mass campaign planning	VectorWorks	400,000		Nationwide	Assistance for continuous distribution system at health facilities (including training, printing) and planning the 2018 mass campaign
SUBTOTAL - ITNs		1,872,000	1,152,000		
Indoor Residual Spraying and Entomological Monitoring					
Increase NMCP entomology capacity and entomological monitoring	IRS TO6	500,000		Nationwide	Provide training, equipment and supplies for NMCP entomology technicians, including insectary support and support for entomology sentinel site monitoring and resistance testing
Technical assistance for vector control activities	CDC	29,000		Nationwide	Two visits to assist with training and to monitor planning and implementation of vector control activities
SUBTOTAL - Entomological Monitoring		529,000	0		

Malaria in Pregnancy					
In-service training and supervision for health care workers at ANC facilities	FARA	450,000		Bong, Nimba, Lofa	At the facility level continue in-service training and supervision of health workers for malaria in pregnancy; community outreach (MOH activity is nationwide with our contribution covering 3 counties)
Improve quality of care and adherence to standards for MIP	CSH	100,000		Bong, Nimba, Lofa	Strengthen QA/QC and quality improvement through technical assistance for supportive supervision at county and facility level for improving MIP practices; support the Liberian Board of Nursing & Midwifery to integrate MIP activities into practical training activities and support quarterly joint monitoring and supervision visits of six training sites for certified midwives
Improve quality of care and adherence to standards for MIP	TBD – Technical assistance for non-focus counties	200,000		12 non-USAID focus counties	Strengthen QA/QC and quality improvement through technical assistance to enable effective training and supportive supervision at county and facility level for improving MIP practices
SUBTOTAL - MIP		**750,000**			
TOTAL PREVENTIVE		**3,151,000**	**1,152,000**	**0**	
CASE MANAGEMENT					
Diagnosis & Treatment					
Procurement of RDTs	TBD-Supply Chain Contract	742,000	742,000	Nationwide	Procure 1.4 million RDTs to help fill gap

Activity	Mechanism	Amount	Amount	Location	Description
Procure laboratory supplies	TBD-Supply Chain Contract	100,000	100,000	Nationwide	Procure laboratory supplies, including reagents, for health facilities and national reference lab
Procure ACTs	TBD-Supply Chain Contract	650,000	650,000	Nationwide	Procure 1,000,000 ACT doses for public and private facilities and community treatment
Procure severe malaria medications	TBD-Supply Chain Contract	140,816	140,816	Nationwide	Procure treatments for severe malaria
Capacity development and supportive supervision for facility-based health workers in malaria diagnosis and in prompt and appropriate treatment of malaria	FARA	550,000		Bong, Nimba, Lofa	Continue support to health facilities for early and accurate diagnosis of malaria cases and appropriate and prompt treatment (MOH activity is nationwide with our contribution covering three counties)
Technical assistance for capacity development and supportive supervision for malaria diagnosis and case management	CSH	305,000		Central, Bong, Lofa, Nimba	Support NPHRL, NDU, and NMCP with technical assistance to enable effective training and supportive supervision at county and facility level for improving malaria diagnostics and case management; support laboratory/diagnostic training costs for up to ten students to complete laboratory tech certification (nationwide placement)
Technical assistance for capacity development and supportive supervision for malaria diagnosis and case management	TBD – Technical assistance for non-focus counties	400,000		12 non-USAID focus counties	Strengthen QA/QC and quality improvement through technical assistance to enable effective training and supportive supervision at county and facility level for improving malaria diagnostics and case management

Activity	Funding source	Amount	Geographic area	Description
Support capacity development of community-based health workers in prompt and appropriate treatment of malaria	FARA	550,000	Bong, Nimba, Lofa	Continue support for appropriate and prompt treatment and early referral of malaria cases, with an emphasis on iCCM
Technical assistance for iCCM scale-up	PACS	200,000	Central, Bong, Nimba, Lofa	Support MOH at central and county level to scale up iCCM, and support service delivery grants to civil society organizations to accelerate scale-up
Technical assistance for iCCM scale-up	TBD – Technical assistance for non-focus counties	300,000	12 non-USAID focus counties	Strengthen QA/QC and quality improvement through technical assistance to enable effective training and supportive supervision for iCCM
Technical assistance to support private sector health facility scale-up	CSH	100,000	Bong, Nimba, Lofa	Support for strengthening malaria case management in private sector facilities
Technical assistance to support private sector health facility scale-up	TBD – Technical assistance for non-focus counties	100,000	12 non-USAID focus counties	Support for strengthening malaria case management in private sector facilities
Technical assistance for malaria diagnostics	CDC	10,000	Nationwide	Technical assistance visit to support efforts of the NMCP to review diagnostic guidelines and improve the rollout of malaria diagnostics
SUBTOTAL - Diagnosis & Treatment		**4,147,816**	**1,632,816**	
Pharmaceutical Management				
Support to extend the LMIS	CSH	100,000	Nationwide	Implement revised LMIS and improve availability and use of consumption data at county and facility level

Activity	Partner	Budget		Location	Description
Strengthen supply chain management (central level)	TBD-Supply Chain Contract	450,000		Nationwide	Support new NDS warehouse operations, ongoing mentoring to SCMU, supervision, forecasting, and quantification in line with revised Supply Chain Master Plan
Strengthen supply chain management (county/district level)	TBD-Supply Chain Contract	400,000		Bong, Nimba, Lofa, Margibi, Montserrado	Expand support to county depots and CHSWTs to rationalize commodity management, storage, supervision distribution, and reporting in line with revised Supply Chain Master Plan
Monitor antimalarial drug quality	PQM	150,000		Nationwide	To help strengthen LMHRA drug quality testing and sampling
Regulation and rational use of pharmaceuticals	CSH	50,000		Central	To help strengthen LMHRA, Pharmacy Board & MOH systems for pharmaceutical regulation
SUBTOTAL - Pharmaceutical Management		**1,150,000**	**0**		
TOTAL CASE MANAGEMENT		**5,297,816**	**1,632,816**		
HEALTH SYSTEM STRENGTHENING/CAPACITY BUILDING					
Technical assistance to strengthen management, leadership and planning capacity of NMCP	TBD	450,000		Central and other 12 counties	LTTA from 2 consultants to strengthen NMCP's management and oversight capacity both internally and externally at central level as well as TA for supportive supervision with the CHTs

Activity	Partner	Amount	Counties	Description
Support for strengthening NMCP and CHT capacity for program management	CSH	130,000	Central, Bong, Nimba, Lofa	Support to the central MOH/NMCP and CHTs to strengthen cross-cutting health systems functions to improve management & governance of the health system, and support decentralization
TOTAL CAPACITY BUILDING		**580,000**		**0**
BEHAVIOR CHANGE AND COMMUNICATION				
Interpersonal communication and BCC	FARA	400,000	Bong, Nimba, Lofa, Margibi, Montserrado	Implement integrated interpersonal communication activities, including health care worker training, to promote all aspects of malaria interventions
Support for BCC through community health services interventions / interpersonal communication, TA for mass media communications	PACS	200,000	Central, Bong, Lofa, Nimba	Disseminate messaging for all malaria interventions, including a focus on BCC for LLINs, iCCM, and testing prior to treatment, including private sector.
Support for BCC through community health services interventions / interpersonal communication, TA for mass media communications	TBD – Technical assistance for non-focus counties	400,000	12 non-USAID focus counties	Disseminate messaging for all malaria interventions, including a focus on BCC for LLINs, iCCM, and testing prior to treatment, including private sector
TOTAL BCC		**1,000,000**		**0**
MONITORING AND EVALUATION				

Activity	Funding Source	Amount	Location	Description
Strengthen data collection and dissemination for decision making (national level)	CSH	200,000	Central	Improve the triangulation of malaria data from HMIS, household surveys and partner reports to inform decision making at the central level; strengthen malaria reporting in HMIS; improve translation of HMIS data to strengthen malaria programming at the central level
Strengthen data collection and use (county level)	CSH	100,000	Bong, Nimba, Lofa	Support county health management teams to collect data through the HMIS and utilize the data to track malaria trends in the health facilities in each county and to incorporate community data from gCHVs in the revised DHIS2 system
Strengthen data collection and use (county level)	TBD – Technical assistance for non-focus counties	200,000	12 non-USAID focus counties	Support county health management teams to collect data through the HMIS and utilize the data to track malaria trends in the health facilities in each county and to incorporate community data from gCHVs in the revised DHIS2 system
DHS 2019	TBD	200,000	Nationwide	Malaria contribution to planning for 2019 DHS
End-use verification tool	CSH	100,000	Nationwide	To support NMCP in the implementation of End-use verification tool
Therapeutic Efficacy Monitoring	TBD	100,000	Nationwide	Support *in vivo* drug efficacy monitoring of first-line antimalarials in two sites
Technical assistance for M&E	CDC	20,000	Nationwide	Two technical visits to support monitoring and evaluation activities
TOTAL M&E		**920,000**	**0**	

STAFFING AND ADMINISTRATION

In-country staffing and administration	CDC/USAID	1,051,184	0	Monrovia	Salaries and benefits, as well as administrative-related costs of in-country PMI staff, and support of cross-cutting and administrative support activities
TOTAL STAFFING AND ADMINISTRATION		**1,051,184**	**0**		
GRAND TOTAL		**12,000,000**	**2,784,816**		

www.ingramcontent.com/pod-product-compliance
Lightning Source LLC
Chambersburg PA
CBHW081239280526
45787CB00006B/2724